FINANCIAL MANAGEMENT

A study of Small Business in North-Eastern Region of India

FINANCIAL MANAGEMENT

A study of Small Business in North-Eastern Region of India

Ashim Kumar Das

AKANSHA PUBLISHING HOUSE
NEW DELHI-110002

AKANSHA PUBLISHING HOUSE
4649-B/21, Ansari Road
Darya Ganj, New Delhi - 110 002
Email: ektabooks@yahoo.com
Ph.: 23263193/9811582579
Fax : 011-23263193

FINANCIAL MANAGEMENT : A study of Small Business in North-Eastern Region of India

First Published 2006

ISBN 81-8370-052-7

PRINTED IN INDIA

Published by M.P. Misra for Akansha Publishing House, New Delhi and Printed at Aryan Enterprises, Delhi

Dedicated
to
Professor Nikhil Bhusan Dey
whose continuous quidance
and
support has been my inspiration

CONTENTS

PREFACE

Small Business units play a significant role in the Indian Economy not only in generating employment opportunities but also in dispersing production across regions and sectors. However, most of these units are neither competitive in the market nor are they professionally managed. In today's market economy, small business units have to sustain themselves on their own competitive strength attained through professional management of these units. In the market there are no concessions and compromises; there is only survival through competition and professionalism. Competitive strength and commercial viability of a business organization, whether small or large, depends on the way it is managed. The owner-manager of a small business is often confronted with many odds, finance being a major hurdle. Finance is the life-blood and critical factor of any fledging business and in small business it is also scarce; hence the small business depends for its very survival on the efficient and effective management of finance. Appropriate management of the financial resources of a small business enterprise is probably the major means to sustain the competitive edge of that business. It is in this context that the present study of the impact of financial management tools and techniques on the management of small business units in the context of north-east India assumes significance.

Financial Management: A Study on Small Business of North-Eastern Region of India is a partially revised version of the dissertation submitted by me to the Assam University,

Silchar for doctoral degree in 2004. The study is a pioneering attempt in the research on financial management of small business in the north-east region and its strengths and weaknesses arise from this fact. My research work, spread across six years, was supported and sustained by many individuals and organizations and my work would remain incomplete without a note of appreciation here. I would like to thank Prof. Nikhil Bhusan Dey of the Department of Commerce, Assam University, under whose able supervision this thesis was completed, for his priceless guidance, tireless efforts, constant encouragement and constructive criticism during the entire tenure of the research. I am proud to have been associated with him in the past many years. As the study depended on primary data gathered from small business owners from all the north-eastern states, I must admit that their cooperation and response to the questionnaires provided a rich background in shaping my ideas on various pertinent issues relating to financial management of small business. I also would like to acknowledge the valuable support, guidance and resources received from Mrs. A. M. Nayak of the University of Birmingham, U.K. and Mr. Dibyojyoti Bhattacharjee, Department of Statistics, G. C. College, Silchar. As for organizations which came to my aid, I would like to mention the North-Eastern Council (NEC), Shillong for a much-needed financial assistance for research, and NISIET, Hyderabad; NEDFi, Guwahati; SISI, Silchar; SIDBI, Guwahati; Assam University Central Library; Gokhale Institute of Economics and Politics, Pune; NIBM, Guwahati for academic resource support. I also cherish in fond memory, the affectionate encouragement of my parents, brother, sister and a long list of friends throughout the research period. A special note of thanks goes to Dr. Gurudas Das, Department of Humanities and Social Sciences, National Institute of Technology, Silchar for motivating and helping me to revise this dissertation for publication and thanks are due also to my publisher.

The book is an in-depth and pragmatic guide for transforming small business enterprises to take the road to success. Besides identifying the problems that ail small businesses in the field of financial management, especially in the north-east region, the study gives a bird's eye view of the present practices of these units and presents a step-by-step roadmap to tackling the challenges of financial management in small businesses professionally. *Financial Management* has a broad coverage of all the pertinent aspects of financial management of small business, like record keeping, working capital management, day-to-day cash management, inventory management, preparation of financial statements etc.

I hope that the book will be found useful, to the owner-managers of small businesses; to the academicians and students working in the area of small business and entrepreneurship, future entrepreneurs and the policy makers.

ASHIM KUMAR DAS

LIST OF TABLES

CHAPTER ONE
INTRODUCTION

Small Business development as an issue has become increasingly important in recent years in both developed and developing countries (Roy and Hutchinson, 1983). Substantial money and energy world-wide has been invested in support services for the small and mid-sized enterprises (SME) sector, as interest has grown in the development of small enterprises (Bolton Committee, 1971; International Labour Organisation, 1992). For example, The World Bank alone has lent over US $3 billion between 1978 and 1989 to foster a healthy growth in this sector in developing countries. Although, it will be impossible to give one to one clear answer to the question "What makes Small Business so important?" but it is quite well known that the term small business is almost equated with poverty alleviation and new job creation through enterprises and entrepreneurship. According to the survey of the World Bank in March, 1988, giving encouragement to the growth of small enterprises was the best way to benefit the masses or non-agricultural job seekers in the developing countries.

Inspite of long drawn planning efforts the strategy for industrialisation adopted in India's economic policy, such as providing gainful employment to surplus labour, alleviation of poverty, egalitarian distribution of income and wealth etc., could not be achieved successfully. The growing dis-enchantment with the supposed virtues of large-scale economic units, has helped to re-focus attention on the "Small Business".

If we look into the history of the small business, the first known piece of work on small business, describing how bankers loaned money at interest, appeared more than 4000 years ago. Since then, it has spent countless hours creating product and services to benefit the consumers. They flourished in almost all ancient cultures. It is largely through small business the civilization was spread to all four corners of the then known world (Barrow, 1997). Significant innovation by small business in the twentieth century are wide ranging – FM radio, over night delivery, personal computers, Xerography, are just a few examples. The beneficial impact on society of such innovations by small business includes not only lower price and better product quality and services for consumers but also a better quality of life.

The widely held view that many of the human aspects of work are more satisfactorily resolved in small organisational units, than in large ones, does seem to be justified. Job satisfaction is probably greater; people are more involved; they feel their work matters more and is better appreciated (Dewhurst and Burns, 1993). Therefore, in terms of their contribution to the economy at any rate it would seem they need to be encouraged.

Economic Importance of Small Business

Small, independent business is the traditional source of local and national economic growth as SSI contribute to nearly Rs. 6.5 lakh crores (40% of gross industrial value and 7% of GDP) in Indian economy. On the other hand Small Trading which contribute nearly Rs. 44,200 crores worth of value added annually to the country's economy (NSSO Report, 1997). Different studies have also shown that most of the new jobs created in this country come from small business. Therefore Micro-enterprise (Small Business) development is an essential and important factor for generating employment and encouraging economic growth in developing countries (Chuta and Liedhotm, 1975; World Bank, 1978).

Danziger and Weinberg (1986) stated that in spite of twenty years of increased spending, the level of poverty in underdeveloped countries has not declined. Education, employment and training initiatives have provided only small gains. They concluded that not enough is known about how to improve the education and employment prospect for the poor and that international assistance to developing countries needs to address more directly the economic needs and potential for self-improvement programs for the poor. Alternative strategies are needed to reduce unemployment and redistribute economic opportunities and benefits among regions and social groups within developing countries (Miller and Kirschetein, 1988).

The interest in and importance of micro-enterprise development among economic planners and international assistance agencies stem from the need for more direct assistance to the alleviation of poverty (Neck, 1977). In contrast to 'top down' economic planning and implementation, micro (small) enterprise programs are based on several 'bottom up' development premises which include the need for : *Harper, 1984, James and Rose Ackerman, 1986*

1. Self-employment opportunities among the poor;
2. Employment which is labour intensive rather than capital and education intensive;
3. Economic growth based on small scale business initiatives;
4. An economic base from which to foster business expansion;
5. The use of natural resources in the economic development process;
6. Development strategies that assist in the transmission of economic initiatives and opportunities from the informal to the formal sector;
7. Economic development opportunities for indigenous population as opposed to 'alien minorities' within a

developing country's social and economic structure;

8. Poverty alleviation through new sources of income;
9. "An incubator environment" from which indigenous services and technology can be nurtured for expanding a country's economic base;
10. Technology adaptation to indigenous resources;
11. Development of entrepreneurial skills and talents.

Small Business units are even more important to economy of developing countries in a functional sense, which include :

a. Interdependence of Business

No modern business is an entity in itself (Baumback, 1988). It must buy from other firms and sell either to different business owners or to consumers in competition with a great many other business. This means that there is a place for everyone, if any business unit has something worthwhile to offer and is able to offer it in an effective and efficient way. Furthermore, numerous small business enterprises are essential to enable a few large ones to concentrate on those activities where their efforts are more effective.

The fact that our economy, with mass production industries, requires great number of small wholesalers, retailers, distributors and other middlemen must be emphasised. Products of mass production units (Industries) are available in thousands of such remote locations only through the invaluable services provided by small independent merchants/small businesses, otherwise, mass distribution of mass production would be impossible.

It is also apparent that the mass producers of automobiles, farm machinery, TV sets and other electro-mechanical products of our increasingly affluent society are very much dependent on thousands of small, independent service establishments for their repair, upkeep and maintenance of these products. Small business also perform a wide variety of commercial, technical and electrical services both for big business and for any other customers in need of their specialised skill and knowledge.

b. Maintenance of Competition

The importance of competition in a country's economy cannot be denied. In the age of rapid economic changes, competition can be the vehicle of change, through innovation or through improvement. Modern competition appears in many forms : price, credit terms, service, product improvement, product marketing strategy, inter-industry struggles concerning substitution/product development and replacement and so forth. Basically, it is rivalry for consumer patronage (Baumback, 88). This competitive environment in a market economy, insures freedom of independent small enterprises and provides an outlet for individual creative impulses and abilities as well as a livelihood for a large segment of the population. It is the best insurance that the country's economy will remain dynamic and provide a continuous stream of innovation, new ideas, experiments and pioneering efforts in new business ventures. Small owner-managed business enterprises are more innovative than are large, publicly held corporate enterprises because ingenious people working on new ideas that relate to their own profit are motivated in a more direct way (Baumback, 1988). Therefore, if we are to continue our progress in extending more goods and services to an ever increasing number of people, big business alone cannot provide these things.

c. Diversity

Diversity is part of the definition of Small Business (Harmon, 1979) – "We are such capitives of the philosophy of so called 'economies of scale' (through big business) that we frequently neglect the more important value of diversity". While big business may be valuable small business is vital. Small Business develops components and ideas that big business uses in its products. Small Business offers services big business cannot accommodate. Small firms train workers who help big firms solve their problems. Small organisations contribute to the community in ways big business cannot.

All these functions/factors of small business point to the most vital feature of our economic system - diversity. It keeps our economy strong and receptive to innovation. Diversity is stimulated by the opportunity for profit (Harmon, 1979). This create a chain reaction as they recirculate in the economy. A person (owner-manager in case of business enterprise) cannot eat profit, nor do profits evaporate and drift away. Profits are reinvested in the market, in better equipment or an increased investment in the form of inventory or in savings account. But in every case, they provide investment capital that increases productivity and raises the standard of living.

d. Small business Firm improve society

It is the small business firm running in an unorganised sector without any management structure that typically hire/ engage, employees of marginal ability (unskilled labour). This term might apply to teen-agers seeking their first job. These individuals often cannot find employment with larger units. Another social benefit from small business is that of leadership training that the young people get in a more practical business environment.

Small business are vital to the nations defence effort. Both the diversity and dispersion of small business add skill more strength to defence because no enemy could conceivably bomb (destroy) all of the nation's productive capacity (Harmen, 1979).

Finally one cannot overlook the psychological contribution of the small business firm. Small Business operators (owner-managers) are optimists by nature, which is one of the important characteristic of an entrepreneur. If they did not believe in themselves and their nation, they would not be in business (Harmen, 1979). The optimism has a certain buoyant effect on workers and communities as they some time becomes the role model of younger generation. In these days of high level of unemployment, personal dissatisfaction/disaffection, country's population needs all the optimism and confidence we can generate – small business is one of the instrument in this direction.

The economic importance of small business was supported by many, at different time in different parts of the world. During the struggle for independence in India, Mahatma Gandhi – "Father of the Nation", has been keen on the protection and expansion of traditional, mainly rural, household enterprises. Another stand of thinking has been shaped by the Report of the Ford Foundation Team (Government of India 1954) which emphasised the role of modern small-scale units as an industrial structure.

In 1973, the publication of Ernest F. Schumacher's study "Small Is Beautiful : A study of Economics as if people Mattered", helped recast the public image of small business in contemporary industrialised societies through the newly proposed concept of "intermediate technology". Schumacher favoured intermediate technology for low-developed countries as it require low equipment cost. Such a technology necessiates regional approach to development and suggest work place should be cheap, method of production should be fairly simple, production should be located in those areas where most of the people live. The oil crisis of the early 1970's and the economic stagnation that followed, prompted rising expectations towards the mysterious power of Small Business ..., as if it could magically step in as a creator of new jobs, a seedbed (or incubator) of new technology, a pool of dynamic entrepreneurship free from rigid bureaucratic vices and even provide the momentum for the revitalization of local communities (Odaka and Sawain, 1990).

The economic argument in favour of small business were considered in the Bolton Committee Report (UK, 1971), which reaffirmed the importance of small business and given reason for doing so. These were that small enterprises provide an outlet for entreprenurial talent; they are most suitable where the optimum production size is small; play an important role as specialist suppliers to large companies; add variety and choice for consumer; act as a check on monopoly power; provide a source of innovation; are a breeding ground for new industries and act as base for new larger companies.

There has recently been a tendency in developing countries to take the benefits of "intermediate technology", which involves smaller business units (Ray and Hatchinson, 1983). This is due to the growing awareness in favour of small business and the problems involved in transplanting larger and heavy technological industries from developed countries. Commenting against transplanting such technologies from developed countries, J.H. Boeke, a development economist pointed out that "we shall do well not to try to transplant the tenden, delicate, hot-house plant of western theory to tropical soil, where an early death awaits them". In many cases such a transplantation has resulted in many undesirable consequences in the form of replacing existing traditional indigenous industries, creating wide spread unemployment; more and more reliance on developed countries – thereby incurring heavy burden of external debts. The painful impact of these consequences ultimately transfer to the shoulder of general population.

Today most of the countries are suffering from huge economic depression and thereby economic growth slowed down. In this crucial juncture small business can act as a shock-absorber for these depressed economics. It has a "flexible element" in the economic growth (Odaka and Sawai, 1990). In ever changing economic climate, Small Business in different countries have demonstrated vitality and high level of adoptability as they thrive everywhere and continue to seize upon new business opportunities. It is therefore, that small business which adjust itself with the new requirement of the economy and at the same time they will successfully help to revitalise the stumbling economies.

Besides unemployment, most of the developing countries are facing many chronic problems – like, capital market may be inefficient or non-existent, the ability to mobolise savings via banking system may be deficient, educational facilities may be lacking, the supply of physical resources in terms of transportation, suitable premises and power are not sufficient according to the demand. In addition, developing countries may have social and political structures which are not conducive to industrial and firm sector growth (Ray and Hutchinson, 1983). So to overcome these problems, developing and underdeveloped countries may encourage small business.

Small Business have acted as a reservoir of traditional manual skill, which are not necessarily needed in big business houses with high capital output ratio. Today this small business has often resulted in economic dualism, where relatively big organisations having imported technology exist with small indigenous concerns typically operated by means of labour intensive traditional technology. In the words of Inc. Magazine (USA) "The world has changed, in short and small business along with it. Where once it was a sleepy appendage to the corporate sector, it now stands alongside it – and in some cases well out in front of it.".

The development of small business is regarded a vital for economic upliftment of emerging economics (ILO, 1990). One ILO (International Labour Organisation) study reveals that, share of employment in small business enterprises, in various industrial groups, roughly about 30 to 40 percent were found to be engaged in manufacturing, construction, trade and commerce, transport and services in developing countries – such as India, Pakistan, Bangladesh ... to count a few in recent past (Maurya, 2001).

In response to the increased attention to small business development, International Bank for Reconstruction and Development (The World Bank) has been putting more emphasis on employment creation in urban areas through assistance to small business, relatively labour intensive enterprises. The ILO for the first time organised the World Enterprise Forum in Geneva in December, 1996, in order to create a business environment conducive to the growth and development of small business. The Committee on Job Creation recommended that the member countries should adopt policies to promote a state economic environment as regard information, interest, taxation, employment and stability and remove constraints to the development and growth of small business.

So, there are many reasons for promoting the small business in developing countries. Development efforts such as this particularly needed to address the needs of the poor and unemployed who could succeed on their own if given an opportunity (Sharma, et. al. 1990). Small Business plays a critical role in the growth and development of local and regional economies. It is through systematic direction of technical support and assistance that indigenous small business enterprise can flourish.

Economic importance of small business in a developing country like India are much more than innovation and invention. Those business have been a vital source of absorbing unaccountable number of persons at places in semi-rural, semi-urban, urban and metropolitan areas, where expeditiously most productive and viable economic activities are done by them in keeping with local demands of goods and items of mass consumption (Maurya, 2001). This is because small business required low capital and low level of barriers to entry. Infact, it is often easier for man/woman to go into small business for themselves than to find an employer. Today, they are so vital that few if any part of the global economy could go on without its products and services. It thrives every where.

In India, besides unemployment, we are facing many chronic problems like poverty, lack of proper education, health, non-existence of efficient banking system and capital market etc. The supply of physical resources in terms of transportation, suitable premises, availability of adequate power etc., are the vital problems. To overcome these unsolved problems the country may encourage small business, which shall bring in a balanced regional growth and their problems could be solved.

The development of the small business may also produce far-reaching social changes in the country. It has been estimated by the sociologists that 53 percent of the Indian population would be under 38 years of age, that means the younger segment of population would become a major constituent of our total population. Hence, there is the greater need for chanalising the resurgence and potentialities of youth of our country in constructive direction (Barpujari, 2002).

Establishment of small business unit, would provide the Indian youth their fruitful opportunities for self-expression and for increasing their material well-being (Barpujari, 2002). Country's younger generation feel frustrated because they do not have assurance that their education and scientific talents would be fully utilised. So their active participation in the small business units would ensure job satisfaction for them. Increasing the small and medium sectors of our economy would strengthen the backbone of society and also curb, social unrest in the country (Barpujari, 2002).

Some time, small business has been criticised for its economic vices, like rat-race competition, the exploitation of employees through low wage, child labour, poor working condition, lack of quality control, environmental pollution and so on. But the other side of the coin, supports the development of small business. As they can act as a shock absorber for a depressed economy like India, it has a flexible element in the economic growth (Odaka and Sawai, 1990). They are characterised by the relatively labour intensive choice of production method, which contribute to the society by enhancing the employment capabilities of skilled and un-skilled, educated and uneducated labour forces which may otherwise remained unutilised. The opportunity to enter into business through small venture, by the new generation, shall cultivate the entrepreneurial spirit in the economy. While giving tribute to these new-entrepreneur U.S.

Congressman John Lafalee said "Entrepreneurs are economic visionaries whose efforts consistently help fuel our nation's economic growth. They are the Pied Pipers of tomorrows corporations, the leaders who will pioneer new products and jobs and create new exports".

Statement of the Problem

Financial Management control is vital for the success of a business whether small or large. Therefore, good financial records must be constantly maintained in business if it is to have effective financial control (Pickle and Abrahamson, 1990). Sound record keeping and analysis can generally increase the possibility of solving many unseen problems early. Financial Management comprises essentially the planning and control of financial resources, that is money. To be a good owner/manager, one has to cultivate the art of analysing and interpreting financial statements, which are prepared using money as a measure. To prevent their units from spinning 'out of financial control', a small business owner "should start with good control system right from the beginning so that there is constant knowledge about what is going on" (Peters and Waterman, 1994).

So, proper financial management is essential for operation of a successful small business units. The present study, therefore, set out to identify the level of awareness, the general practices and uses of financial management tools and techniques by Small Business owner/manager in running their units. Small Businesses with only one major decision-maker, are in a unique position as only at this size a firm can manage without having to communicate information to others (people in and outside the business). To match the present pace of change in the business environment and maintain a competitive edge, the owners/managers of small business units must know personally in correct form the present position of his/her business. So, for small business enterprises to flourish, more sophisticated accounting tools can not be a luxury (Soral and Jain, 1994).

We have taken up this study because we believe, and the survey of growing literature on financial management of small business units reveal, that there is wide gap between theory and practice of financial management. They hardly find the existing financial management techniques of any use. There are seldom few written documents or records. As a result, a great majority of small business units do not survive long and remain in operation with low level of efficiency.

Several studies have been undertaken on the financing aspect of small business, but very limited work has been undertaken to research indepth into the management aspect of finance (money) which act as a 'life line' of a business. Without ongoing control of financial resources, we would not be able to spot profitability concerns or opportunities" say's William Mc Bride. "Operating without a detailed financial analysis would be like trying to play poker blind folded".

Financial Management aspect of a small business is often assumed as most neglected area, because owners/managers of the small enterprises do not understand its functions and utilities for business survival and growth. As a result, the simplest items, like keeping track of cash or tracking exactly how the business is doing, get lost (Peters and Waterman, 1994). Waterman (1994) recommends that small businesses owners/managers should "look at this kind of information as a proactive management tool, not merely as historical information". One classic study (Potts, 1992) on financial management and control techniques in small business concludes that "the clearest and most startling distinctions between successful and discontinued small business lies in their approach to the uses which can be made of accounting information".

As it is commonly believed that the very survival of the business depends on its ability to make profit, but it does not happen by accident. It requires careful planning, a lot of sound management and control techniques. Ian Peter, Head of Small Business, National West Minister Bank says "success does not happen, it needs to be planned. Business planning is about business understanding their own risks and how they are going to manage them to achieve their objectives .... It's about being in control". A financial expert Eileen Davis says, "Small Business that does not establish sound controls at the start are starting themselves up to fail".

The purpose of the present study is to discover whether small business units which do not have to collect information for dissemination to others, have enough information to pursue their goals. Each firm which is owned and managed by single individual and with unlimited liability, the owners/ managers must have every incentive to apply the appropriate level of effort and to make the correct utility maximizing decision. This is because the owners/managers of small businesses would personally bear all the costs associated with the mistakes. As Benjamin Frankin said, "beware of little expenses; a small leak will sink a great ship". So a little mistake may cost huge money. Thus, small enterprises cannot dare to make mistakes. Properly kept financial records and their analysis make it possible to eliminate mistakes.

Notwithstanding the abundance of prescriptive literature on financial reporting and analysis in small business enterprises, there is very little empirical evidence to support recommendations made in the literature. Furthermore, theory development in the area is minimal and cannot adequately support the recommendations (McMahon and Davies, 1994). The exploratory study described in this research work, attempts to find empirical justification for the prescriptions in the theory of financial management.

From a sample (non-random) of small business enterprises, the study seeks possible associations between historical financial records and analysis practices and overall financial control and performance of small business in North-Eastern Region of India.

Recognising the importance of financial management

practices in general and management of small business in particular, this study is an attempt to explore and highlight the status of financial management practices of small business units in North-Eastern India; and particularly the small business owners/managers perceived awareness; and the use of selected financial management tools and techniques for financial control. The result of this study is expected to highlight area of accounting and financial management that require attention from the private and public organisations interested in development/growth of small business enterprises in India and North-East in particular with special reference to Assam.

Review of existing literature

A rapidly growing literature on the financing and financial management of Small Businesses suggest that there is a considerable number of reasons for believing that the financial management of small businesses is or should be qualitatively as well as quantitatively different from that of large enterprises (LeCornu, et. al. 1996).

There are obvious institutional differences such as regulatory influences, sources and types of finance, and forms of financial assistance. In addition, quite distinctive inherent characteristics of small enterprises/businesses are likely to lead to differences. Levin and Travis (1987) and Petty and Bygrave (1993) discusses the following : (a) In large enterprises there is frequently separation between management and ownership, whereas small enterprises are more likely to operate as extensions of their owner-managers; (b) small enterprises may be faced with fewer investment and financing options; (c) small enterprises (Business) often suffer from 'resource poverty', particularly of a financial nature; (d) starting from a smaller base, small enterprises are generally more likely to experience problems associated with the consequences of growth, such as liquidity pressure; (e) small enterprise financial management is inevitably more dependent on the ability of a single individuals than is the case in large enterprises; (f) the absence of a well-formed market for ownership stakes in small enterprises is likely to impact on their financial management.

On the motivations of small business enterprise owner-managers, three important messages appear to emerge from the empirical literature (Hankinson, 1977; D'Amboise and Gasse, 1980; Ray and Hutchinson, 1983; Bolton 1971; Cooley and Edwards, 1983). It is suggested that owner-managers of small businesses –

(a) may not have a single overriding aim like wealth maximization but rather their intentions are likely to be numerous and complex;

(b) have motive which are unequivocally non-monetary and

(c) have considerable freedom to pursue objectives, monetary or otherwise.

Keats and Bracker (1988) suggested that 'performance may have a different set of meanings for small firms than for large firms". The melding of ownership and management in small enterprises allows the goals of the owners to become the goals of the firm (Naffziger, et. al. 1992). In this way, it appears that behaviour and decision making in small enterprises are unequivocally attached to the personal motivations of the owner-managers. The Bolton Committee (1971) reported that the need to attain and preserve independence was the fundamental motivation in most small enterprises.

Other researchers concur with this view and assert that both financial and personal independence are frequently pivotal factors in the decision to initiate a small business (Pandey and Tewary, 1979; Perry, 1980). Brigham and Smith (1967), and Boyer and Roth (1978) argue that owner-managers may be satisfied with a lower rate of return since they have control of operations and the advantage of working for themselves.

It would appear from the literature that there are a number of distinguishable characteristics of small enterprise

(Business) which are not considered in the maxims of modern finance theory and that may account for the masked risk-return relationship which has plagued new areas of small enterprise research (LeCornu, et. al. 1996). Lack of diversification of their human investment (or capital) may prevail due to the owner-manager's total involvement in the management and operating activities of the firm.

Owner-managers of a small businesses have considerable freedom to pursue and derive satisfaction from non-financial motivations.

This may cause the pursuit of decision outcomes and financial control that rationally diverge from those considered to be wealth-maximising, which is the traditional financial goal of the firm. But, as Hutchinson and Ray (1986) indicated, growth can result in financial stresses such as cash-flow difficulties and excessive use of debt. This financial problem create a critical need for improved financial control which came about through an upgrading of financial reporting and analysis systems.

The present research is a contemporary work on financial management uses and practices and its impact upon the performance and growth of small business enterprises. Numerous articles, reports and research papers have appeared on this topic, but very limited work has been done on the financial management aspect of small business in India and more particularly in North-Eastern states. The literature survey is basically confined to the abstracts of different reports (Government and Non-Governmental Agencies etc.), academic and institutional works (published and unpublished) and other mentionable addition so far been made by various contributors in the national and international level on this fertile subject.

A substantial body of prescriptive literature has evolved dealing in whole or part with use of financial tools and techniques by the small business enterprises. In recent times, the books written on financial management for small business emphasise the importance of developing skills in reading and interpreting historical financial statements to monitor financial health and progress (Black, 1950; Harman, 1979; Tungale, 1952; Rausch, 1982; McMahon, 1986; Meredith, 1986; Walker and Petty 1986; Barrow, 1988; Scarborough and Zimmerer, 1993; Kuchl and Lambing, 1994). In journals of small business, some articles strongly advocate use of financial analysis skills for small business units (Mayo and Rosenbloom, 1975; Konstans and Martin, 1982; McMahon and Davies, 1994).

A number of recent publications deal with the distinguishing characteristics, problems and growth of Small Scale Industries in India. Most of these works highlight the importance of small business in the country's economic development and also details the changes required in the organization and management of such enterprises in order to survive and prosper (Ramakrishna, 1962; Mathur, 1979; Dey, 1980; Bala, 1988; Vepa, 1988; Satyanarayan, 1989; Mali and Deka, 1995; Rudramuthy, 1997).

Several studies have been undertaken to determine what financial ratios are used by owners/managers of Small Business to monitor their businesses (Lewis and Toon, 1986; Holmes and Nicholls, 1989; McMahon and Davies, 1991). Attempts have been made in some cases to measure business success as function of knowledge and use of these information. However, these studies have been on large sized small businesses.

A contemporary research work on small business at West Midland, U.K., (Nayak and Greenfield, 1994) shows that firms which do not do well, is not because of lack of business records and lack of awareness of key business factors, but due to the lack of adequate accounting knowledge and proper financial records. Comprehensive financial reporting and analysis should generally lead to improved financial control and that this in itself could significantly increase the chances of a small enterprise prospering through growth (McMahon and Davies, 1994).

It has been observed that there is wide gap between theory and practice of management accounting in case of small business. On the other hand financial accounting system is based on the traditional "Mahajani" system and is incomplete in nature. No systematic form of financial statement analysis were noticed (Soral and Jain, 1994). Large number of small and tiny business units do not maintain even proper books of accounts, which are necessary for proper control of the business. Past experience and intuition plays important role in financial decision-making. Among the other factors, the non-use of financial tools and techniques for financial decision-making has resulted in a variety of financial problems, which the small units faces (Vinayak, 1987). Non-existence of financial analysis and accounting practices has been observed in other studies also. There were problem in increasing the financial assistance to small industries by the Financial Institutions due to lack of accepted accounting practices and financial management (Rao, 1984).

It is also observed that, those who ignore the financial aspect of their businesses run the risk of becoming just another failure statistics. To reach profit objectives, the small business owners-managers must be aware of the firm's overall financial position and the changes in financial status that occur over time (McMahon and Holmes, 1991).

Another study (LeCornu, et.al. 1996) has thrown light on the financial objective of small business units. They found that financial management of small enterprise is or should be qualitatively as well as quantitatively different from that of large enterprises. Small Business financial management is inevitably more dependent on the ability of a single individual or small number of individuals. It also appears that behaviour and decision making in small enterprises are unequivocally attached to the personal motivations of the owner-managers. The absence of a well-formed market for ownership stakes in small enterprises is likely to have an impact on their financial management.

Rice and Hamilton (1979) in their study found that small businessman employed a multidimensional, stochastic, non-quantitative decision process, which are primarily informal in nature. All the theories governing business operational decision making presume that the owner/ manager is a rational, cogent and calculating individual and he should use "scientific decision making". However the finding was that for a majority of small businessmen decisions were the result of 'experience', 'intuition', or 'guesswork'. This implies that in small business units scientific decision making process does not take place.

A study was conducted by Narayanan, et.al., (1987) to know to what extent small business financial problems and practices were responsible for the poor recovery, sticky and irregular bank loans. The authors have studied such loan accounts of several branches of SBI and UCO Bank. The study has tried to show how non-use of financial management tools and techniques have led to non-payment of loan amount.

Another study by Holmes and Nicholls (1989) concluded that the amount and nature of accounting information prepared or acquired is dependent on number of operating and environmental variables like business size, age, industrial grouping, owners/managers education. The findings of the study also revealed that most owners/ managers engage an accountant to prepare statutory accounts, additional information (of non-statutory nature) tends to be prepared within the business.

New economic policies have introduced a host of changes throughout economy. Business life for owners/managers has changed considerably. To ensure their continued survival, there is a need for increased emphasis on management development activities. People may be called upon to act in new ways, attend to new concerns and master new-concepts and skills if they are to thrive in the reconstructed economic environment (Linower and Dixon, 1992).

Recently there has been a major focus on accounting information as an aid in planning and control for small businesses. This effort has resulted in the utilization of modularized contribution margin income statements as an aid to decision making and policy formulation. It is important that small business owners/managers have an awareness of this approach which is designed to provide better visuality and understanding of their financial situation (Dunne, et.al., 1980).

Maximization of profit or 'surplus' is the primary objective of an enterprise. Efficient and scientific management of finance in an enterprise is of prime importance for achieving that ultimate goal. In practice, the matter of production or materials quality or marketing in the ultimate analysis, relates to financial issues (Sen, et.al., 2001). All-out efforts are needed for applying the tools of financial management to the enterprises in a scientific manner in the interest of injecting fresh confidence and restoring the financial health of the organisation.

The results of another study (Siop and Ahmed, 2000) shows that there is a big gap between the owners/managers, awareness and the use of financial management control techniques. It seems small businesses enterprise owners/managers are venturing into business without proper financial 'know-how'. Even owner/managers who are aware of financial management control techniques are somehow restricted from using them to effectively manage their enterprises.

Gap in the existing literature

The existing literature strongly support the argument that in small business, Financial Management is the key issue. It not only increases the success rate but also affects the level of performance.

Several studies (Sharma, 1976; Barooah, 1980; Dey, 1980; Baishya, 1986; Deb, 1993; Smith, 1997) have been undertaken in North-Eastern Indian states viz., Arunachal

Pradesh, Assam, Manipur, Meghalaya, Mizoram, Nagaland and Tripura to determine the underlying problems of small businesses in the field of financing, marketing, infrastructure etc. However, no study has been conducted exclusively so far on the awareness and uses of financial management tools and techniques by small business units. This aspect of small business has been left untouched and has not been extensively researched.

The present study, therefore, is expected to contribute towards filling the present gap in the knowledge, prevailing in the area of small businesses in general and their financial management practices in particular. The study will also examine the impact of uses and non-uses of financial management tools and techniques on the survival and growth of small business units of North-East India in general and Assam in particular. The purpose of this study is to discover, whether small business units, which do not have to collect financial information for dissemination to others, have enough information to pursue their goal.

Rationale of the study and its social relevance

The last decade has seen a rapid growth in the number of small business units. They are the only source of self-employment and act as an economic shock-absorber. It is more so in the North-Eastern India, because here small business is the only ray of hope for large number of people (educated/uneducated) for self-employment. North-Eastern India is industrially backward, having poor infrastructural facilities and agriculture is also subsistence in nature, and hence the only gainful economic activities for survival is "Small Businesses". Therefore, Small Business units have become a highly topical area for research.

The present study has been undertaken keeping in mind the importance of small business units in the socio-economic development in North-East India and to deal with unemployment problems in this region.

Financial Management is a vital aspect to the success

of a small business units. In North-East India no study has been undertaken so far to look into financial management practices in small business units. It was felt that a survey which looked at large number of small units in North-East might reveal interesting insights on how they gather/record and use the tools and techniques of financial management.

The topic is thus considered to be socially relevant and useful for small businesses management. The findings of the present study is likely to throw light on the mechanism to arrest the failure/sickness in small business sector in this region in particular and the country in general.

Objectives of the study

Major Objectives of the present study are as follows :

(a) To assess the level of perceived awareness of the owner-manager of small business units about tools and techniques of financial management.

(b) To examine the pattern of managerial use of the financial management tools and techniques by the small business units.

(c) To evaluate the impact of Financial Management practices on the survival and growth of the units.

(d) To extend some pragmatic suggestions based on the findings of the study.

Research Queries

Proposed research work aims to address the following queries :

Q1. Whether the owner/manager of Small Business units are aware of the Financial Management tools and techniques ?

Q2. Whether they make uses of the same in managing their businesses ?

Q3. Whether use of appropriate Financial Management techniques can aid the growth and survival of the Small Business units ?

Research Methodology

The main objective of the present study is to examine the level of awareness and practices of financial management tools and techniques by the owner-managers of small business units/firms in North-East region of India.

The present research study is "Exploratory" in nature. The exploratory research advocated by Petty (1991) relies on 'simply and subjectively observing phenomena in their natural setting and deriving theories that fit the analysis of the data'. It reflects the belief that this is a valid approach to theory development in a field where there is presently insufficient accepted theory to guide the research (Abdel-Khalik and Ajinkya, 1979). Therefore, major emphasis in such (Exploratory) study is on the discovery of ideas and insight (Kothari, 1996). In the present case, this applies to financial management and analysis in general and to these activities in small businesses in particular. Such research may rely on a relatively small, non-random sample, can often be characterized as descriptive and/or associative and thus without pretensions to causality; and may employ non-parametric and distribution – free statistical methods and possibly techniques for structural escalation of data (McMahon and Davies, 1994).

There are indications that the broad data analytic approach to research outlined is finding increased acceptance in the literature concerned with small business.

The present research work, therefore, calls for field data or primary data from natural setting. The primary data were collected with the help of interviewer assisted questionnaire. The questionnaire so prepared included questions about general as well as specialised aspect of record-keeping, decision making etc.

(a) Sample selection

The importance of small business units in the economy of North-Eastern region of India is well-known fact and need not to be reiterated. The present study, therefore, restricted itself to the study of small business units located in North-Eastern states of India with special reference to Assam.

For the present research the working definition of small business units/firms, which fulfilled the following quantitative characteristics were considered :

(I) All Small Scale Industries (SSI) registered and unregistered (as defined under SSI Policy, 1991 as amended in 1998)

  (a) Manufacturing unit – investment limit in plant and machinery upto Rs. 10 million.

  (b) Ancillary unit – investment limit in plant and machinery upto Rs. 10 million.

  (c) Tiny sector including service sector – investment limit upto Rs. 5 lakhs.

(II) Small Trading units (Whole seller/retailer) who run firms with under fifty (50) employees (with full time/part time; skilled/unskilled labourers).

While selecting the sample units, the following points were taken into consideration :

  (a) Since one of the objectives of the study was to evaluate the impact of financial management practices on the survival and growth of the firms/units, an attempt was made to choose those units which were in operation at the time of survey, for a period of atleast two years so that an actual picture of record keeping and financial management practices and their uses for the business decision making by the owner-manager can be ascertained.

  (b) At the time of selection of small business units for the present research study, due care has been taken to select small businesses who fulfil the quantitative characteristics for small business units as stated above.

  (c) This type of study required in-depth interviews

and prolonged discussions for which several visits to the units and a lot of time and willing co-operation of the respondents were needed. An attempt was, therefore, made to select only those units where the investigator had either some approach or the entrepreneurs (owner-manager) were willing to cooperate.

Due care has been taken to include in the sample different segments of the small business population. The segments are :

(i) Manufacturing units

(ii) Service units

(iii) Trading units

(b) Size of the sample

As the universe is very large, it was decided to take a sample size of around 220 from the entire region keeping in mind the different business segment and different states involved. However, finally 208 duly filled in questionnaire were collected and out of which 191 duly filled in correct questionnaires were processed for the purpose of analysis.

The researcher himself collected field data through interviewer assisted questionnaire from three important states – Assam, Meghalaya and Tripura and for the remaining states like Mizoram, Arunachal Pradesh, Manipur, Nagaland – properly briefed and qualified interviewer were entrusted with the job and sent nearly 120 questionnaires to them.

The state wise sample position shows that 62 p.c. of the respondent were from Assam and 38 p.c. were from other North-Eastern states. Efforts were made to include at least 10 sample from each states other than Assam. The interview has taken place during the early 2003 to early 2004 at a time when the business climate was stable in this region.

Due care has been taken to select sample units which were representative in nature in terms of business sectors and size of the units by applying judgement sampling method. Small business units were selected from seventeen (17) major commercially important places of the region including Assam.

(c) Statistical Tools Used

The data were collected with the help of a structured questionnaire along with a loosely structured personal interview schedule (guide) for the entrepreneurs. A pilot survey was conducted within small group of small business units in Silchar Town of Assam to know the tendency of the entrepreneurs (owner-managers) in answering the questions and the type of data which were made available by them. Consequently, the questionnaire was modified suitably and a set pattern of question was emphasised through the questionnaire as well as in the in-depth interviews. Sampling was non-random judgement sampling was used so that data are representative and purposive in nature.

Since it was not possible to meet the assumptions underlying parametric statistical testing, the study used appropriate non-parametric tests of association as the sample collection was based on Judgement Sampling.

Chi-square (χ^2) is an important non parametric test and as such no rigid assumptions are necessary in respect of the type of population. We require only the degree of freedom for using this test, as a non-parametric test. Chi-square (χ^2) can be used

(i) As a test of goodness of fit.

(ii) As a test of independence.

χ^2 (Chi-square) is calculated as follows :

$$\chi^2 = \sum \frac{(o_{ij} - e_{ij})^2}{e_{ij}}$$

Where O_{ij} = observed frequency of 'i' th now and *j* th column
e_{ij} = expected frequency of 'i' th now and *j* th column

As a test of goodness of fit, χ^2 (Chi-square) test enables us to see how well does the assumed theoretical distribution fit to the observed data. When some theoretical distribution is fitted to the given data, we are interested in knowing as to how well this distribution fits with the observed data. The chi-square test can give answer to this. If the calculated value of χ^2 is less than the table value at a certain level of significance, the fit is considered to be a good one which means that the divergence between the observed and expected frequencies is attributable to fluctuations of sampling. But if the calculated value of χ^2 is greater than its table value, the fit is not considered to be good one.

As a test of independence, χ^2 test enable us to explain whether or not two attributes are associated. We generally proceed with the null hypothesis that two attributes (for example, age of the business and uses of financial management tools) are independent, which means that age of the business has no effect in using financial tools and business performances. On this basis we first calculate the expected frequencies and then work out the value of χ^2. Now, if the calculated value of χ^2 is less than the table value at a certain level of significance for given degrees of freedom, we conclude that null hypothesis stands, which means that the two attributes are independent or not associated. But, if the calculated value of χ^2 is greater than its table value, our inference then would be that null hypothesis does not hold good which means that two attributes are associated and the association is not because of some change factor but it exists in reality.

It may be mentioned here that, χ^2 (chi-square) is not a measure of the degree of relationship or the form of relationship between two attributes, but is simply a technique of judging the significance of such association or relationship between two attributes (Kothari, 1996).

Steps involved in applying chi-square test are :

(i) First of all, we have to calculate the expected frequency on the basis of given hypothesis or on the basis of null hypothesis. The expected frequency for any given cell is worked out as under :

Expected frequency of any cell =

$$\frac{\text{(Row total for the row of that cell) X (column total for the column of that cell)}}{\text{(Grand total)}}$$

(ii) Obtained the difference between observed and expected frequencies and find out the squares of such differences i.e., $(o_{ij} - e_{ij})^2$.

(iii) Divided the quantity $(o_{ij} - e_{ij})^2$ obtained by the corresponding expected frequency to get $\frac{(o_{ij} - e_{ij})^2}{e_{ij}}$ and this was done for all the cell frequencies or the group frequencies.

(iv) Then, to find the summation of $\frac{(o_{ij} - e_{ij})^2}{e_{ij}}$ values or

$\sum \frac{(o_{ij} - e_{ij})^2}{e_{ij}}$ This is the required χ^2 valuc.

The χ^2 value obtained as such were compared with relevant table value of χ^2 and then inference were drawn as stated above.

Besides the above tests the study also used average, percentage, rating scale etc. whenever required to present the data. Chart and diagram were also used.

Limitations of the study

The study is likely to have following limitations inspite of our best efforts.

(1) As the present research study is exploratory in nature and is distinguishable from the scientific method,

which should be theory based, where we first develop the theory, build our hypotheses from the underlying theory, then we test empirically (Petty, 1991). At this stage of the investigation into the financial management practices for small business the exact questions and measurements necessary for hypothesis testing was not yet identified. Hence hypothesis testing could not be done. The aim of the present research was to describe the phenomena and includes some preliminary statistical testing without any reference to causality ...., it provides a relatively inexpensive theory – building stage prior to the commitment of significant resources to a large sample (Le-Cornu, et. al. 1996).

(2) As the widely-acknowledged authority on exploratory research Tukey pointed out, it is still true that exploratory methodology can only be a beginning, a base from which subsequent confirmatory research can begin. With this in mind, the present research might be judged on the basis of the questions it raises regarding potential significance for further investigation, rather than upon answers it may provide.

(3) The dynamics of small business enterprise growth are inevitably complex and affected by many factors other than financial management. It was not possible to control for these other influences in the exploratory study with a limited sample size.

(4) Given small sample size and the lack of homogeneity among small business population and the selection bias, there is a need for caution in making generalisation based on its findings.

(5) As no official definition was there for small businesses in India, a working definition for the study was framed taken into consideration – qualitative and quantitative parameters/characteristics.

(6) The sampling and data collection methodologies

employed inevitably impose limitations on interpretation of the results of this study. There is no indisputable assurance that the non-random (as study employed judgement sampling), final sample was representative of the small business in the region as a whole. The accuracy and completeness of the data collected relied heavily on the ability and skills of interviewers and also the co-operation of owner-manager interviewed.

(7) Because of the sensitivity of financial information, there was no attempt to determine the actual amount of credit, debit, total amount of borrowing, capital invested, net profit/losses by the participating small business units.

(8) A further limitation of the present research work is that the methodology used could not gauge all the factors influencing the responses, such as the moral standing and social beliefs of owner-manager. These considerations on financial management and reporting practices, limits the internal and external validity of the study.

CHAPTER TWO

SMALL BUSINESS IN INDIA : A CONCEPTUAL FRAMEWORK

Looking into the socio-economic importance of small businesses in developing economy like India, here at this stage question may arise as to what constitutes a "Small Business". This is an important problem which arises in any discussion of small business development and growth. It is important in empirical studies to adopt a plausible definition of smallness and in comparative studies to use a consistent definition, in practice it is probably true to say that a small enterprise is easier to recognise than to define. Measures used in research studies are often based on quantifiable variables such as number of employees, sales, turn-over, profitability or net assets.

In India, Small Scale Industry (SSI) and Small Industrial Policies have been a widely known phenomenon. From the First Industrial Policy Resolution, 1948, later on the Industrial Policy Statement, 1977, 1980 and 1991 with New Policy Measures for Small Tiny and village enterprises, reiterated that the main thrust should be on the effective promotion and development of SSI (Table-2.1).

The policy framer also recognise that despite all the promotional measures through policy direction, the SSI (Small Scale Industries) must be appropriately defined with a view to determining the types of small business units

Table – 2.1

Evolution of official definition of SSI in India

Change Over time year	Investment criterion Normal small-scale units	Ancillaries	Employment criterion
Up to 1958	Fixed capital in vestment up to Rs. 0.5 million	Fixed capital in vestment up to Rs. 0.5 million	Employment up to 50 workers if using power or up to 100 workers if not using power
1959	The value of machinery was taken as the original price paid irrespective of new or old machinery.	The value of machinery was taken as the original price paid irrespective of new or old machinery.	Employment up to 50 workers if using power or up to 100 workers if not using power
1960	Gross value of fixed assets up to Rs. 0.5 million	Gross value of fixed assets up to Rs. 1.0 million.	Employment Criterion dropped

INVESTMENT LIMIT (APPLICABLE ONLY TO PLANT AND MACHINERY, RS. MILLION)

	Normal	Ancillary	Export-oriented small units	Tiny units
1966	0.5	1.0	–	–
1975	1.0	1.5	–	–
1977	1.0	1.5	–	0.1
1980	2.0	2.5	—	0.2
1988	3.5	4.5	–	–
1991	6.0	7.5	7.5	0.5
1997	30	30	7.5	2.5
1998	10	10	7.5	2.5

* For an ancillary unit there is a requirement to supply at lest 50 p.c. of its product /services to other under taking.

* Export-oriented units are under obligation to export at least 30 p.c. of the annual production by the end of the third year and onward from the year of commencement of production.

* A SSI unit cannot be controlled or owned by or be a subsidiary of any other industrial undertaking.

*(**Source** : NPC Research Division and Kashyap (1995) for details until 1991.)*

which needed special support. It was considered necessary to develop an appropriate classificatory definition for SSI units for the first time under the Industrial (Development and Regulation) Act, 1951. Since then, the definition underwent many revisions during the last 50 years, where cut-off point has shifted from a workforce to an investment criterion (SIDBI, Report on SSI sector, 1999). In the Table No.-2.1, the periodic revisions in the official definition of SSI sector in India are summarised.

In India, inspite of many positive shifts during the last 50 years, the concept of Small Scale units, has remained more protective in nature whereas in other developed countries like in U.K. it has become more open. It is observed that in India, Small Scale Industry (SSI) covers mainly the manufacturing sector or industry related service sector only but it left untouched a major segment of small business in the field of trade and commerce (Biswal, et. al., 1997).

Small traders and other commercial enterprises, which has been left out in the present definition, are the major creator of new independent jobs and sells most of the products made by big manufacturer to the ultimate consumers. These unorganised sector of business activities contribute nearly Rs. 44,220 crore worth of value added annually to the country's economy, employing 222 lakhs workers in nearly 145 lakhs small trading enterprises (NSSO Report on Small Trading Units in India and their basic characteristics: 1997). Due to heavy pressure of population in the country, where the number of job seekers has increased manifold and hence the opportunity to get employed, has become very difficult, it is the genius of "Small Business" to offer the greatest hope to the greatest number of people. Therefore, it is the need for the present socio-economic environment, to have different sectors in a vast country like India is perhaps inevitable, otherwise it may be unmanageable (Biswal et. al., 1997). In this direction framing a comprehensive definition of 'Small Business' may be taken as supportive measure for the development and growth of Small Business in the country.

When we look into the definition of Small Scale Industry (SSI) in India, what prevails here is only the concept of small scale, ancillary and tiny industries which are related to the historical value of the investment in plant and machinery (SIDBI report on SSI sector, 1999). But if we look into the other developed/developing countries, Small and Medium Enterprises (SME's) are defined on the basis of both quantitative and qualitative elements. When it defines quantitatively, labour/employment is an omnipresent criterion for determining the size of the units in these countries (SIDBI, 1999). In a labour surplus economy like India, employment as a criterion to identify a 'Small Business' shall be the most relevant development.

In the age of liberalised market economy, the survival of the fittest is the main 'mantra'. In the competitive environment, quality control and automation are the need of the hour, which require bulk investment in plant and machinery and other intangible assets. So imposing restriction on investment limit, through definition of Small Scale Units in India, shall ultimately restrict technological development and growth of this sector. Therefore, investment on plant and machinery should not be taken as the only yard-stick to identify a small/medium enterprise. On the other hand labour/employment criterion may also be considered. The prevailing definitions in some countries are listed in (Table-2.2).

While defining a 'Small Business' qualitatively by different reknowned authorities in various countries like, the Committee on Economic Development (USA); Small Business Administration (USA); Bolton Committee Report on Small Business; U.K. (1971), U.K.'s Companies Act, 1989; The Wiltshire Committee, Australia (1971); etc. has identified the following parameters or organisational characteristics to define a 'Small Business' :

- They are independently managed and controlled by the owner/manager. In some cases salaried persons are also appointed as manager.

- The area of operations of such firms are usually local.
- They are not dominant in the field of operation, hence the firm can not normally influence the market price.
- Capital is usually supplied by the owner/manager, however borrowed capital is also used to finance such business.

Although we have many concrete definition of 'Small Business', propounded by different authorities in different countries, but unfortunately in India we do not have any such precise definition of 'Small' and 'Medium' size enterprises (SME). Many a time SSI (Small Scale Industries) and tiny sector definition given in various Industrial Policies (Government of India), has been quoted as 'Small Business' by many authors. It is observed that in the present SSI definition the terminology for 'Small Business' is equally haphazard. Hence 'Small' is often extended to 'Micro' and 'Medium' Size units. By same token 'Business' is frequently substituted by 'Company', 'Concern', 'Enterprise', 'firm' or even 'industry', depending upon the preference of the author.

The term Small Scale Industry (SSI) evokes different meaning for different agencies also (SIDBI, 1999). The Planning Commission (Government of India), views the entire Village and Small Industry (VSI) sector as a part of the SSI sector. The National Sample Survey Organisation (NSS) under the Central Statistical Organisation (CSO), defines the entire industry sector in terms of organised and unorganised segments as well as in terms of industrial enterprises run by household and non-households. The Central Excise Department on the other hand, distinguishes SSI on the basis

Table – 2.2
Definition of Small and Medium Business unit in different countries

Name of the Country	Category of Industry/ Business	Criteria
China	SME	Depends on product group, investment ceiling 30 million Yuan (US$8 million).
Germany	SME	No size definition. Craft firms are members of Craft Chambers and are defined by types of business and the qualifications of master craftsman. About 95 percent of small firms have an employment of less than 20 workers.
Japan	Manufacturing	Less than 300 employees and capitalisation less than 100 million yen.
	Wholesale Trade	Less than 100 employees and capitalisation less than 30 million yen.
	Retail Trade and Services	Less than 50 employees and capitalisation less than 10 million yen.
Mexico	Micro	Less than 15 employees and gross Income Sales less than US $1,75,000.
	Small	15-99 employees and gross Income Sales less than $1,75,000.
	Medium	100-249 employees and gross Income Sales less than $1,75,000.
Malaysia	SMIs	Employment less than 75 full time workers or with a shareholder fund of less than RM 2.5 million (US$1.0 million).

(Condt...)

Name of the Country	Category of Industry/ Business	Criteria
	Sis	Manufacturing establishments employing between 5 and 50 employees or with a shareholders fund up to RM 500.000.
	Mis	Manufacturing establishments employing between 50 and 75 full time employees or with shareholders fund between RM 500,000 to Rm 2.5 million.
Taiwan	SMEs	In manufacturing, paid up capital less than NT$60 million or number of regular employees not exceed 200.
	SSEs	In manufacturing, regular employees not to increase 20.
South Korea	Small	Less than 20 Employees
	Medium	20-300 employees. In some categories upto 700 employees with assets of up to US $7,00,000 (SO bn Won)
France	Small	Ownership of the firm must be private, the owner should assume a direct financial, technical and managerial involvement in the firm. The number of employees must be under 500.
Sweden	Small	The limit commonly set at either 50 or 200 employees. However, other quantitative and qualitative criteria are sometime used.
USA	Small	Employees fewer than 500 persons.

*(**Source** : SIDBI Report on SSI Sector - 1999 and other publications).*

of the annual turnover of the units. The Reserve Bank of India (RBI) adopts an expanded definition of SSI which includes traditional industries as well.

Given the inherent characteristic of high degree of heterogeneity, diversity and complexity in the present definition, 'Small Businesses' can be best understood when it is viewed according to general macro-economic condition. Recognising the limitations in the 'Small Business' definition in India and to include all the economic constituent of small business i.e. trade, industry and commerce, to remove the present definitional ambiguity about the terminology of 'small' 'medium', 'micro-business' units, a new approach is needed for determining the size of the Small Business in India.

New approach of defining Small Business in India

For designing an appropriate and accepted definition of Small Business we have to take into consideration, the New Policy Measures for Small, Tiny and Village Enterprises (1991), Small Trading Units (defined by NSSO) in India and also definitions and concept developed by renowned international authorities in various countries like, the Committee on Economic Development (USA), Small Business Administration (USA), Bolton Committee Report on Small Business (U.K. 1971), U.K.'s Companies Act, 1989, the Wittshire Committee (Australia, 1971). Therefore, to remove the definitional ambiguity and to evolved a brought policy framework in India, the concept of defining small business may be worked out after taking into consideration both quantitative and qualitative characteristics which may be as follows :

(I) Quantitative Characteristics

While defining of Small Business units/firms, which fulfilled the following quantitative characteristics may be considered :

(1) All Small Scale Industries (SSI) registered and unregistered (as defined under SSI Policy, 1991 as amended in 1998)

(a) Manufacturing unit – investment limit in plant and machinery upto Rs. 10 million.

(b) Ancillary unit – investment limit in plant and machinery upto Rs. 10 million.

(c) Tiny sector including service sector – investment limit upto Rs. 5 lakhs.

(2) Small Trading units (Whole seller/retailer) who run firms with under fifty (50) employees (with full time/part time; skilled/unskilled labourers).

(II) Qualitative Characteristics

In addition to the above quantitative characteristics, the following qualitative aspects may also be considered :

(a) They are independently managed and controlled by the owner-manager, who has responsibility for the firm's principal decisions. In some cases salaried person are also appointed as manager.

(b) The area of operation of such units/firms are usually local.

(c) They are not dominant in the field of operation, hence the firms can not normally influence the market price.

(d) Capital is usually supplied by the owner manager, however borrowed capital is also used to finance such business.

This qualitative characteristics (economic definition) makes a great deal of sense. It has actually three parts :

1. Independence
2. Personalised Management.
3. Market share.

Here, Independence means that the owner has control of the business himself.

Personalised management is the most important characteristic factor of all. It implies that the owner actively participates in all aspects of the management of the business and in all major decision-making processes. There is little delegation of authority. One person i.e. owner-manager, is involved when anything material is concerned. But if one owner-manager of small business has to manage and control everything, what a wide range of skills he must need ! Unlike the chief executive of a large corporation who can employ a secretary, a financial advisor/director, a cashier/treasurer, an accountant etc.; all well informed in their own professional fields and all willing and able to advise him. The small business proprietor has to be himself, a man for all.

The characteristic of a small firm's share of the market is that it is not large enough to enable it to influence the prices or notional quantities of goods sold to any significant extent.

All this unique characteristics provide ample support for the belief that small businesses are unique; and that a research about their financial management practices is justified.

Different segment of small business

Small businesses predominate in all private sector of the economy. The relative importance of the small business firms, differs considerably from one type of business to another. We shall consider here in our study only the major areas of business activity – the manufacture of products; the distribution of products of all kinds and the rendering of services.

Manufacturing

Despite the predominance of the larger firm, there is still much room in which the small manufacturing firm can maneuver. Big industry is more effective in well-established industries where large markets for low-unit-cost products exist; where technology and mechanisation have been developed to high degree of efficiency, but where huge capital investments are required and where standardisation and simplification are desirable policies (Baumback, 1988). However, the mass-production system is often dependent on the small production plant/factory for supplies and components. It is the very existence of the large manufactures, in fact, that provides the smaller manufacturers with many of their opportunities.

It is observed that our large manufacturers/producers are essentially assemblers of the products of thousands of small specialised manufacturers. Thus it is the manufacture of producers' goods (products made for other manufactures) wherein most of the opportunities exist for the small, independent enterpriser.

Opportunities exist for the small manufacturer in local consumer markets also. Some of the more common examples of 'local' manufacturing are printing shops, bakeries, bottling plants, manufacturing of plastic/wooden product, food processing industries etc. These are the ubiquitous industries present in every community/places of commercial importance in a district, that provides needed products for local consumption. As a community grows or population increases, so also do the opportunities for the small local manufacturer.

Merchandising/Retail Trading

Retailer or merchandisers are middlemen in the channel of distribution who sell products to the ultimate consumers. It is apparent from different studies in different countries that retailing remains largely the bailiwick of the small independent business enterprises. Small firms also predominate in wholesaling.

Just as the mass-production system is dependent on the small parts manufacturing plant, so also is it dependent on the small merchant. Each retail store handles from a few hundred to well over a thousand different items/products of small and large manufacturers. It is observed that most of the consumer goods are distributed through wholesale establishments and to the last consumer by the small retail stores, the majority of which are small businesses. Obviously, the small merchant plays a major role in gathering together countries wealth of production and making it available for use (consumer) (Baumback, 1988).

Service Activities

Service businesses offers hundreds of different kinds of services to the consumers, to government agencies and non-profit organisations and also to other business houses. They are run/staffed by technically trained/skilled people with skills for hire. Most of the common types of service businesses perform work on goods owned by the customer or upon the person of the client. With some exceptions in the transportation, communications and public utilities field, the dominant characteristic of the service business is its small size.

Most of these businesses require only a small initial investment and depend heavily on close personal supervision. The barber shop for example, has never achieved mass production, nor has the watchmaker. Neither the finisher of old/new furniture nor the restorer of metal objects can do work mechanically beyond certain preparatory steps.

Therefore, the role played by service industries in the economy is becoming increasingly larger. An important factor contributing to this growth is that the purchase of services is taking an increasingly larger proportion of the consumer's money. Higher incomes and the increased purchasing power available to the average individual has provided the consumer with funds to hire someone else/some services to perform personal and business services.

The growth of the service industry can also be attributed to the fact that, since most services are difficult if not impossible to mechanise or automate, productivity per worker is not increasing as rapidly in this industry as in most other sectors of the economy (Baumback, 1988). This is particularly evident in business services, repair services, personal services and amusement and recreational services.

Who is an Owner-Manager ?

In the present research study, we generally used the

owner of the small business units as the "owner-manager" of the organisation. It needs to be emphasised that while we will talk about the small firm owner-manager throughout the text, this term can include anyone from a self-employed shopkeeper to a chief executive (who may own high/ maximum proportion of the firm's capital) of a high technology enterprise with substantial assets in the business. The term (owner-manager) also includes individuals with many different objectives, ownership interests and motivations. The present study do not identify the small firm owner-manager as necessarily an entrepreneur.

CHAPTER THREE

NORTH-EASTERN REGION OF INDIA : A BRIEF PROFILE

North-Eastern Region of India : A brief profile

The North-Eastern region of India comprises of seven (7) states viz, Arunachal Pradesh, Assam, Manipur, Meghalaya, Mizoram, Nagaland, Tripura.

This region is also known as the land of 'seven sisters'. These states were organised by carving out some specific areas from the state of Greater Assam from time to time. Total area of the region is about 2,55,168 sq.km. North-Eastern region of India comprises about 4 percent (38.49 million : 2001 census) of the country's population spread over 8 percent of its land area. There are 75 major population groups and sub-groups that speak about 400 different languages and dialects. About 70 to 80 percent of the population depends on agriculture for its livelihood. Another unique feature of the region is its high rainfall, which ranges between 3000mm to 12,000mm.

Region with vast potential

The North-Eastern region of India is endowed with vast reserves of natural resources. The region contributes about 50 percent of India's annual tea production. Oil is a thriving industry and the region is endowed with huge timber and water resources. The region is also rich in manpower resources with a literacy rate that stands much above the national average. The North-East accounts for one-third of the country's total hydro-power potential. At 60 percent PLF, the proven potential is about 36,000 MW against the country's total of 84,000 MW. Added to that is the vast potential that this region has in terms of tourism.

Proximity to countries such as Bangladesh, Myanmar, Bhutan and China brightens the North-East's prospects of trade and commerce with these nations, especially at a time when nations of the South East Asian region are liberalising their economies. Sectors such as energy, cement, food processing and trade and commerce would be prospective areas of cooperation with these countries. ASEAN's market of 500 million consumers, is for all purposes, at North-East India's doorstep.

North-East India : Natural Reserves

Natural gas	190 bn. cubic metres
Coal	909 mn. tonnes
Hydroelectric potential	36,000 MW
Oil	513 mn. tonnes
Limestone	4,933 mn. tonnes

Promotion of small business activities in trade and industry is a policy response to meet the challenges posed by growing unemployment in North-Eastern states. The small business enterprises have been a vital source of absorbing unaccountable number of persons, where expeditiously most productive and viable economic activities are done by them in keeping with local demand of goods and items of mass consumption. Entrepreneurship through small business would provide the youth of North-Eastern region, their fruitful opportunities for self-expression and for increasing their material well-being. Increasing the small scale sector of industry and trade of this region, would strengthen the backbone of our society and also curb social unrest in the region (Roy, Das and Rakshit, 2003).

To support the growth of small business the Central Government as well as State Governments of this region has, over the past few years offered a number of incentives for setting up of industrial units in the North-East. The new Industrial Policy for the region provides an extension of the Transport Subsidy, at 15 percent Capital Investment Subsidy, 3 percent Working Capital Interest Subsidy, total exemption from Income Tax and Excise Duty for 7 to 10 years and a comprehensive insurance policy where the Central Govt. will pay premiums for upto 10 years.

Inspite of vast natural resources and economic potential, North-East India is struggling with the problems of economic development. The region depends on imports of foodgrains and other products like fish, egg etc. on large scale in spite of vast land mass remaining unutilised in the marshy areas of the plains and particularly in the hills of the region. In the Industrial field, the region has only 1.8 percent of the factories and employed less than 2 percent of the factory workers of the country. Almost every item of mass consumption and every item of conspicuous consumption is imported from the rest of the country (Datta Roy and Baishya, 1998).

Agriculture is based on traditional low technology, subject to periodic ravages of floods and drought in the plains while in the hills terrace cultivation through crop diversification on scientific basis is yet to replace shifting cultivation (Jumming) which actually destroy rich top layer soil and result in the cutting of green forest coverage on a large scale. Thus the entire North-East India is caught up in low productivity in agriculture and low income syndrome.

With the small size of the local market and low income level of the North-Eastern states in India, large scale industrialisation programme would not be applicable. Moreover, the disadvantageous geo-ecological location of these states (in a seismic zone) also come on the way of establishment of heavy industries. Moreover, there are some social and political factors which inhibit the import of capital from outside.

In such a situation, the use of local skills and capacity through small scale units and small business might have stretched the existing potential to a considerable extent. Even certain kinds of highly specialised products of this region on their own merit would find their way to national as well as international market. For example, hand made textile and silk materials, cane wares, wooden products, processed fruits etc. are some of the products which could easily and efficiently be producted in the North-Eastern states and would earn substantial amount of income for the economy. As the population is growing, markets are expanding and consumerism has caught imagination of the expanding middle class, there is an ample scope for trade and commerce in this region's market.

It must be mentioned here that the tribal society in spite of backwardness, does not suffer from any insurmountable cultural obstacles to entrepreneurship development like the 'Eastern' society mentioned in Boeke's theory of dualism. In fact, in many respects a substantial segment of the tribal society in the North-Eastern region in urban and semi-urban areas is more 'Western' than their non-tribal counterparts owing to their contact with the missionaries and progress in education (Bhattacharjee, 1998). It may be mentioned here that in most of the North-Eastern states, literacy rate is more than the national average. It is true that high literacy rate or even progress in general education is no indicator of growth, skill and business enterprise development, but it atleast indicates that the tribal society in the North-Eastern region of India is not averse to change and that the cultural factor is not a stumbling block on economic development in general and entreprenurial growth in particular. The growing number of road-transport operators, servicing shops, hotels, public call offices etc. go to show that the educated youths of the region are not averse to entreprenurial activities of related infrastructure and capital are forthcoming.

Small Business in North-East India

In the field of industries, the large scale units barring a few in Assam, are almost non-existent in the North-Eastern region. A total of 155 large and medium industries were functioning in the region in 1991. Of this, almost 80 percent are in Assam. Although there is potential for developing various resource – based industries in the region, but due to many hard and soft infrastructural problems, large scale industries did not come up in this region.

Therefore, small business would play a dominant role in the region's economy in the years to come. In regard to Small Scale Units (SSI) a total of 9,330 units (in 1998) exist in the region, which account for only 1.6 percent of all India total. The total number of workers employed in these units accounts for 68.6 thousand which forms 1.9 percent of India's total of 3665.8 thousand person (Table 3.1).

In regard to small trading business a total of 4,50,507 units were found in the region (1997) and yearly Gross Value Added (GVA) from these units comes to Rs. 1376.14 crores for the region's economy (Table 3.2) annually.

Table 3.1

Small Scale Industries in North-Eastern States (1998)

States	No. of Units	No. of Employees (000)
Arunchal Pradesh	326	2.8
Assam	4430	34.5
Manipur	2078	10.2
Meghalaya	587	3.8
Mizoram	917	4.2
Nagaland	183	3.0
Tripura	809	10.1
Total in N.E. states	9330	68.6
All India (SSI)	**5,82,368**	**3665.8**

Table 3.2
Small Trading Units in North-East Region of India.

States	Rural	Urban	Total
Arunachal Pradesh	7244	2034	9278
Assam	2,36,722	1,02,223	3,38,945
Manipur	10,311	13,568	23,879
Meghalaya	16,069	5,716	21,784
Mizoram	4,584	5,225	9,808
Nagaland	4,632	6,276	10,908
Tripura	28,063	7,840	35,903
Total	**3,07,625**	**1,42,882**	**4,50,507**

(*Source* : NSS, 53rd Round "Small Trading Units in India and their Basic Characteristics : 1997).

Table 3.3
Yearly Gross Value Added (GVA) for North-Eastern States by Small Trading Units.

(in crores)

States	(Rural + Urban)
Arunachal Pradesh	Rs. 43.72
Assam	Rs. 927.95
Meghalaya	Rs. 70.85
Mizoram	Rs. 41.56
Nagaland	Rs. 27.11
Manipur	Rs. 125.45
Tripura	Rs. 139.50
North-East regions Total GVA	**Rs. 1376.14 (crores)**

(*Source* : NSS, 53rd round "Small Trading Units in India and their Basic Characteristics : 1997).

The states of North-East India – at a glance

Arunachal Pradesh

Arunachal Pradesh is a thinly populated hilly tract on the eastern most part of India, surrounded on three sides by the international borders with Bhutan on the west, China to the north and Myanmar to the east. Towards the south are Assam and Nagaland. The state is predominalty tribal in character. To keep it under a kind of protective cover, the innerline restrictions are inforce to avoid any infiltration of the people from the plains of India.

Assam

Geographically, Assam is shadow of its former self. It has been reduced to one-third of its original size in about 30 years time. Assam continued to loose territory and population step by step as Nagaland, Meghalaya, Mizoram and Arunachal Pradesh were separated from it

Assam situated in the North-East corner of India and is surrounded by Bhutan and Arunachal Pradesh on the north, Nagaland and Manipur on the east, Meghalaya and Mizoram on the south and Bangladesh, Tripura and West Bengal on the west. Only a narrow strip of sub-mountain region of the Himalayas connects Assam with the Indian mainland. The state is divided into three regions – the Barak Valley, the Brahmaputra Valley and Assam Hills.

Number of Enterprises per thousand population

State	No. of Enterprises	Projected population (000) of 1997	Per 1000 population
Assam	**338945**	**25149**	**13.48**

Percentage of wholesale, retail and other trading units in Assam.

State	Wholesale Units	Retail Trading Units	Other Trading Units
Assam	**2.9%**	**90.8%**	**6.3%**

Estimated Gross Value added (GVA) per enterprises in Assam.

State	OATE	NDTE
Assam	Rs. 1840	Rs. 7833
All India (Average)	Rs. 2074	Rs. 9545

- OATE : An business enterprise is run by owner-manager only and is engaged in trading, it is termed as an own-account trading enterprise.
- NDTE : An business establishment employing fewer than six (6) workers is termed as Non-Directory trading establishment.

North-Eastern States at a glance

Name of the state	Area in sq.km.	Capital	Population
Arunachal Pradesh	83,743	Itanagar	8,58,392
Assam	78,438	Dispur	2,22,94,562
Manipur	22,327	Imphal	18,26,714
Meghalaya	22,429	Shillong	17,60,626
Mizoram	21,081	Aizawl	6,86,217
Nagaland	16,569	Kohima	12,15,573
Tripura	10,492	Agartala	27,57,205

Source : Cenus 2001.

Manipur

Manipur has been a Union Territory from 1956 and a full-fledged state since 1972. The state is bounded by Nagaland in the north, Mizoram in the south, Myanmar in the east and Assam in the west. Manipur has been known to the Indian traditions for a long time. The epic Mahabharat tells us how the hero Arjun, the princess Chitrangada and their son Babruvahana was among those who fought bravely in the war in Kurukshetra.

Meghalaya

Meghalaya, was made an autonomous state on April 2, 1970 and a full fledged state on January 21, 1972. It is a mountainous region having Garo, Khasi and Jaintia hills. The state is bounded by Bangladesh in the west and south, Assam at the north and east.

Mizoram

In 1972, it was made a Union Territory and renamed Mizoram from Mizo Hill District. It became 23rd state of the Indian Union on 20th February, 1987. Mizoram in the northeast corner of India, is bounded on the north by Manipur and Assam, on the east and south by Myanmar, on the west by Bangladesh and Tripura.

Nagaland

It was a Centrally Administered Territory in 1957 and was accorded statehood in 1961, but was officially inaugurated on 1st December, 1963. More than 15 Naga tribes inhabit the state. The state is a narrow strip of mountainous territory between Brahmaputra Valley and the Myanmar. It is bounded by Myanmar in the east, Manipur in the south, Assam in the west and north and Arunachal Pradesh in the North-East.

Tripura

Tripura was a state of great antiquity having been ruled by the Maharajas for 1300 years, before its accession to the Indian Union on 15th October, 1949. The territory was made a full state on January 21, 1972. Tripura represents a composite culture with several ethnic groups residing in the state.

The princely state of Tripura is bounded on the north, west, south and southeast by Bangladesh and on the east by Assam and Mizoram states. The state is inhabited largely by ninteen (19) tribes, Bengalis and Manipuri communities.

CHAPTER FOUR

MANAGEMENT THEORY : ITS IMPLICATIONS IN SMALL BUSINESS

Management is an universal phenomenon. Every organisation requires the making of decision, the coordinating of activities, the handling of people and the evaluation of performance directed towards achieving objectives. Lack of proper management invariably results in chaos, wastage of time, money and effort. The productive efficiency of business firms depend a great deal on the quality of management. It has become more important as labour has become more specialised and as the scale of operations has increased. Technological developments have continually created new challenges.

The characteristic of management is the integration and application of the knowledge and analytical approaches developed by numerous disciplines. The task of an owner-manager in a business organisation is to seek a balance among these special approaches and to apply them. Management is an activity that converts disorganised human and physical resources into useful and effective results. It brings order to endeavors by combining isolated events and disjointed information into meaningful relationships. These relationships then work to solve problems and accomplish organisational goals (Terry and Franklin, 1997).

The Meaning of Management

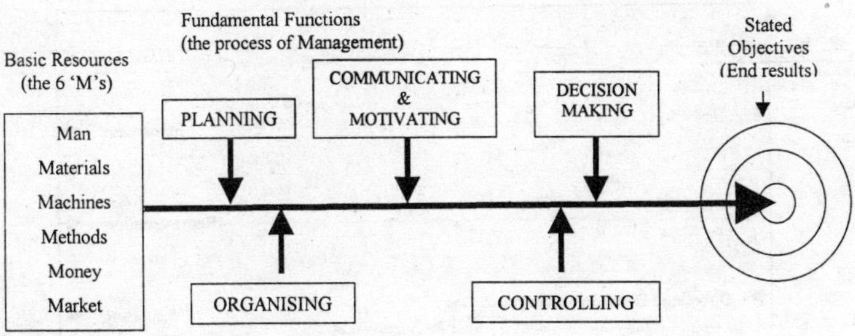

Source : Terry and Franklin (1997).

The process of management to achieve the organisational goals is to identify the basic functions which together makes up the process. Although different authors have given different names for the key functions of management, however, there is general agreement on most of the actual duties of a manager. The main function of management :

(1) Planning

(2) Organising

(3) Directing / Decision Making

(4) Communicating

(5) Controlling.

Besides these main functions, there are some sub-functions of management.

These functions of management are inter-related to each other and constitute the focal process of management. They are required to be carried on simultaneously in the process of management and not in any pre-determined order. William Fox points out that planning, organising and controlling are the organic functions of management. According to him, an organic function is a function which is invariably basic to, and inherent in managerial activity. These functions are performed in each and every situation. No business whether

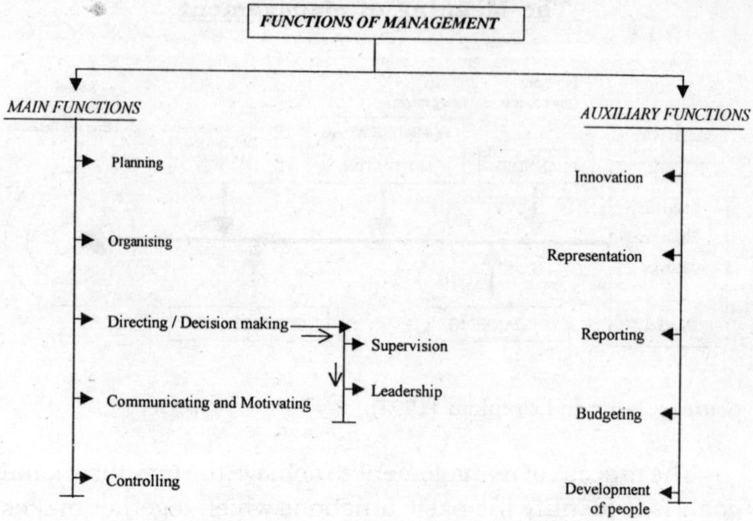

it be small business or big business organisation, can succeed without proper planning and without direction, no plan be put in operation. Better operation and correct performance of business can be achieved only by motivation, proper co-ordination and efficient control of its different activities.

Therefore to achieve the economic objectives, the Small Business owner-manager must successfully perform all the basic management functions in the start up as well as during growth stages of the business unit.

In terms of management functions, achieving the objectives can be expressed on a three step process. The first step involves the careful planning of future needs for funds, both short-term and long-term, through the proper maintenance of an efficient budgeting system. The second step involves acquiring the needed funds from the most economical mix of sources. And the third step is to use the acquired funds in the most efficient manner. This third step is often referred to as the control function of management. If all the functions are properly conducted that may improve future performance of an organisation.

Planning and setting the goal of the organisation

The function of planning implies that goals or objectives of an organisation have been defined. Planning refers to the determination of the line of action to achieve a desired result on goal. It is the process of thinking before performing. Imagination, foresight and sound judgement are required for planning.

Henry Sick has defined planning as "the relevant of information from the past and the present and the assignment of the probable future development so that a course of action may be determined to enable the organisation to meet its objectives."

Planning formally correlates the organisation to its present and future environment. Once the objectives are chosen, the owner-manager has to formulate policies and programmes to achieve them within a certain specified time. He/She has to decide what is to be done, how, when and where it is to be done and who is to do it. Planning is the most important step in the process of getting results by adjusting present actions in view of the established goals. Planning bridges the gap between where we are to where we desire to be in the future. It strongly implies not only the introduction of new things but also sensible and workable implementation. Although the future can seldom be predicted with accuracy and unforeseen events may interface, unless there is planning actions tend to be aimless and left to chance.

Planning therefore, includes determination of the objectives, policies, rules, programmes, strategies, budgets and procedures. The ultimate task of planning is to minimise the risk and at the same time to take full advantage of the available opportunities. Planning eliminates uncertainties and confusion and sets a regular predetermined course of action for the achievement of better and certain results. Proper planning also secures economies in operation.

Good planning must be flexible and capable of adjustment

to the changing circumstances. Planning is necessary in good times as well as in bad times. So planning is a function which every manager has to undertake irrespective of the size and nature of enterprise. Planning generally brings a higher degree of rationality and order into the organisation. The organisation/enterprises with effective long range planning will be able to greatly outdistance their competitors.

Therefore, planning function of management implies that goals or objectives have been defined. For the purpose of the current study the need to define the proper objectives rests on these two reasons.

1. If goals or objectives of the business are unknown it cannot be determined whether or not sufficient information is available to enable planning to take place.
2. Should it be desired to determine a correlation between the amount of management information available to the owner-manager of a small business and the 'success' of the business, this would presumably be the ability to achieve goals.

Current thinking on business goals is of two main stands. First moves from the economic theory concept, that business always attempts to maximise owner's wealth and also suggests that due to bounded rationality and general inertia, businesses satisfy and operate at the level and always search newer options until they find a plan which provides satisfactory profits.

The second option, draws from Organisational theory as every business follow an organisational structure. This theory suggest that in a small business organisation it is impossible to distinguish the objectives of an organisation from the objectives of the owner-manager. These individuals bargain, using the resources they bring to the organisation, attempt to acquire their share of personal satisfaction, be it power, money, interesting lifestyle and so on (Nayak and Greenfield, 1994).

Both these ideas are very relevant to small businesses

as the proprietor (owner-manager) does not have to bargain with other parties within the organisation and does not have to disseminate information to the internal/external parties. So it could be deduced that the objectives of the owner are those of the business too. If this idea is accepted, it is necessary to discover whether the owner has enough information to plan, for the organisation.

The literature strongly supports the argument that, in small business, planning is a key issue. Planning not only increases the success rate (Jones, 1982), but it also affects the level of performance (Schwenk and Shrader, 1993). This idea was also supported by Bracker and Pearson (1986), who identified different levels of performance associated with different levels of planning.

Organising

Organising is the creation of a harmonious structure of authority - responsibility relationship. It is the mechanism through which management directs, co ordinates and controls the business. Main aim of organisation is achieving optimum co-ordination of the function of any business unit. It is intentional in the sense of making sure that all the tasks necessary to accomplish goals are assigned to people who can do them best. So organising is the human relationship in group activity equivalent to social structure. In the words of Fayol to organise an enterprise means "to provide it with everything useful to its functioning – raw materials, tools, capital, personnel". Organising is just like the functioning of the human body, through which the purpose of life is served.

In a large organisation, organising usually relates to deciding who within the business will perform which task and what resources they need to do it. But in a Small Business with only one decision maker it will focus more on ensuring that the information is to hand (Nayak and Greenfield, 1994). Handy in his book "Understanding Organisation", discusses that organisational structure of

Small Business Enterprises are power centric. The organisational structure of Small Business is best depicted as a web – where all authority and power emanating from one individual. There is little bureaucracy but they rely heavily on the central figure and the successor provides the key to continued success or failure. It is a competitive atmosphere, closely controlled from the centre.

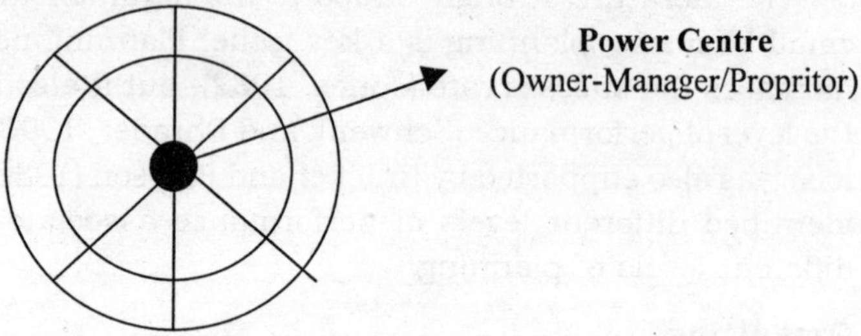

Organisational Structure of Small Business

Directing and Decision Making

The decision-making process is an important and integral part of the management process. Managerial action is largely decision-making. It is the act of choosing from among alternatives. A good decision is based on a choice of calculated alternatives based on judgement. It is the product of deliberation, evaluation and thought process. To make good decisions, manager's should follow a sequential set of steps. If managers do not go through this sequence, they are likely to make a decision that will solve wrong problem rather create new one. Decision making process in an organisation involves the following stages :

(i) Identifying the problem

(ii) Analysing the problem

(iii) Developing alternative solutions.

(iv) Comparing the alternative solutions.

(v) Choosing the best solution

(vi) Implementing and verifying the decision.

Fredickson and Mitehell (1984) defined decision comprehensiveness as the "extent to which an organisation (or individual) attempts to be exhaustive or inclusive in making and integrating strategic decision. According to these authors, a comprehensive decision maker is one who follows a formal rational decision process in which the cause of the decision problem is formally identified and an exhaustive or large set of decision alternatives is developed and evaluated. In implementing this decision process, the comprehensive decision maker attempts to gather as much information as possible using sources both inside and outside of the organisation. In summary, the comprehensive decision maker strives to make the best decision possible through the identification and evaluating of a large number of alternatives.

Small businesses owner-managers are described as decisive and unique individuals who are impatient and quick to respond to organisational problems. Consequently, it would be expected that these owner managers to be less comprehensive in their decision making. For example, entrepreneurs from small business firms would be unlikely to assign formal responsibility for a decision to a subordinate because of limited personnel and their need to control (Borland, 1974). Further, one would expect entrepreneurs to be too impatient and not to have the organisational systems appropriate for following a rational comprehensive decision model involving extensive and exhaustive information gathering and analysis (Smith et. al. 1988).

As small business owner-managers are the individuals who single handedly control the whole activities of his/her organisation. So, and hence is in a better position then big business to identify the actual problem and take proper decision.

Communicating and motivating

Managers spend a major percentage of their time transmitting their ideas to others, orally and in writing. Other managerial functions, especially controlling and organizing, involve communication problem. Communication serves as a linking process by which parts of a system are tied together. It makes possible the managerial process and serves as the lubricant for its smooth operation. Communication helps managerial planning to be performed effectively, managerial organising to be carried out effectively and managerial controlling to be applied efficiently. So providing regular and complete information to different members of an organsiation to ensure that they are able to carry out their job effectively, individually and as a team, is one of the most difficult tasks of management.

Motivation implies securing fullest co-operation of each individual worker for the realisation of the economic goal of the business organisation. Norms of performance laid down under "controlling" may not be achieved simply by "directing" alone. Human needs, desires and sentiments are to be taken into consideration. Motivation is the process of creating in the workers, a will-to-work and to develop a co-operative attitude so that they put in their best. So, motivating participants to work for the benefit of the organisation is a hard task. To effectively respond to participants' communicational and motivational needs requires constant awareness of changes in the organisation and in the roles and attitudes of all participants. These issues (communication and motivation) are less problematic in small businesses as there is either only one or few participants, so that activities and issues can be discussed regularly and a team spirit can be generated.

On the motivations of Small Business's owner-manager, three important messages appear to emerge from the empirical literature, (Bolton Committee 1971; Hankinson 1985; D'Amboise and Gasse 1980; Ray and Hutchinson 1983). They suggest that owner-managers (1) may not have a single overriding aim like wealth maximization but rather their intentions are likely to be numerous and complex; (2) motives which are unequivocally non-monetary and (3) have considerable freedom to pursue objectives, monetary or otherwise.

Frequently cited motivating factors include the need to control one's own life, to have greater flexibility for personal and family life, to achieve a higher position in society, to be respected and to have freedom in adapting one's own approach to work (LeCornu, et. al. 1996).

Keats and Bracker (1988) suggest that "performance may have a different set of meanings of small firms than for large firms". The melding of ownership and management in small business allows the goals of the owner-manager to become the goals of the firm (Naffziger, et. al. 1992). In this way it appears that behaviour and decision making in small business units are unequivocally attached to the personal motivations of the owner-manager.

Controlling

Control within oganisations is a process of monitoring activities to ensure that they are fulfilling organisational goals. The essence of control lies in checking existing actions against some desired results determined in the planning process. As the predetermined criterion should be stated explicitly, for this reason, quantitative statements are usually preferable. In financial management, money value serve as explicit statements of norms. Management use past achievement of the firm in financial term as crude yardsticks for controlling current operations.

In any control system by the management, the measurement of actual performance is the most important element. This step usually requires proper records and appropriate reports which is devised to present information in the organisation that will fit the control system. Prompt reporting of actual performance increases the efficiency of a control system.

Another element of control system involves the study of relationship. Such techniques on financial ratio analysis, trend analysis, mathematical equations and charts etc. can help to the measurements of actual performance by showing the relation of actual experience to the pre-determined (planned/budgeted) criterion. The purpose of comparing past performance with planned performance is not only to determine when a mistake has been made but also to enable the manager to predict future problems. A good control system in an organisation will provide information quickly so that trouble can be prevented in future.

So, controlling involves scanning the environment for means of fulfilling goals, choosing alternative course of actions and subsequently checking whether or not those actions have succeeded. In large business organisations controlling involves defining, co-ordinating and measuring the activities of the various department and members of the organisation. But in case of Small Business unit it will focus more on the resources that the owner-manager (Proprietor) has put into his business, and to measure the effectiveness of his decisions on the day to day running as well as long term decision making (Nayak and Greenfield, 1994).

Bank of America's Small Business Reporter publication entitled "Avoiding Management Pitfalls" cites eight (8) areas of management incompetency that generally lead to small business failure. They are :

1. Downgrading the need for experience.
2. Poor record keeping.
3. Poor cash management.
4. Failure to plan.
5. Misuse of time.
6. Inattention of marketing.
7. Ignoring the human factor.
8. Failure to assume the proper role.

1. Downgrading the need for experience

Most of the small business units are founded on one person's abilities; the owner-manager. If this individual lacks the skills and versatility to either perform or supervise the tanks of finance, accounting, marketing and other aspect of management, the venture is destined for failure.

2. Poor record keeping

Poor financial records create problems in ever fact of the small business; yet the need for a good accounting system is frequently overlooked. A study of unsuccessful small business units showed that all had accounting system so imprecise that the state of the business remained unknown even to the owner. Although a knowledgeable accountant can set up an effective system and keep it going; the owner-manager must understand the financial information derived from the system and be able to use it in decision making.

3. Poor cash management

The failure to maintain a stable and adequate financial position is a serious management error. A "cash poor" firm has little or no bargaining power and must waste a good deal of time struggling to appease creditors.

In the new firm the problem is one of under capitalisation simply not putting enough capital into the venture to really get started. In the going concern, on the other hand, too much capital can get tied up in fixed assets, slow-paying receivables or obsolete inventory, if growth is not properly controlled.

In dealing with the cash flow problem, the owner-managers of small business should prepare their budget and adopt money management techniques to accomplish cost and cash control.

4. Failure to plan

Professional business consultants generally agree that one of the most frequent causes of small business failure they observe is the lack of planning. The rapidly changing market of today demands forward – looking strategies. Well-formulated plans permit the business organisation to take better advantage of opportunities as they arise and head off management difficulties before they become too serious.

Planning is not simply 'thinking ahead'. It involves the establishment of objectives and determination of methods for reaching the objectives. Without these elements the owner-manager of small business is merely indulging in wishful thinking, not planning.

5. Misuse of time

The typical entrepreneur has too much to do in too little lime. Good time management is learning to control the job rather than letting the job control the person. The job objective is to work "smarter", not harder. Proper management of time is a matter of self-discipline. Effective manager's put 'first things first'; they generally rank duties according to their importance.

A critical aspect of time management involves delegating appropriate jobs to suitable persons, to free the owner-manager for the routine, operational duties. A owner-manager who fails to properly delegate can become so involved with everyday activities that important jobs, like planning, etc. often rushed.

6. Inattention to marketing

Sales are the secret to success in any business venture. The best of products, personnel and physical plant is of little use without customers. Unfortunately, some owner-manager of small businesses has the false impression that their products on services will sell themselves. But, the true is, few things sell themselves. Marketing is essential to build customer awareness.

An objective analysis of the firm's products or services, its present marketing effort, the competitive situation and the genuine needs of customers will show the ways to solve sales problems.

7. Ignoring the human factor

Most employee difficulties result from poor personnel administration. Too many owner-managers spend all their time worrying about production, sales etc. and solve personnel problems on a 'crisis' basis. A loyal and efficient work force can be built only if adequate attention is given to hiring, training and managing of employees.

8. Failure to assume the proper role

The success or failure of any business venture depends on the quality of owner-manager. The skills and talents required to be a good owner-manager, change as the organisation changes due to time. The owner-manager's managerial know-how necessary to run a one-man operation in the early years is much difficult from the needs of a growing firm five or ten years down the line.

As the business grows to new stages of development the owner-manager must adopt his/her role. The transition from operator to manager, to execute must be smooth.

The eight pitfalls described are by no means a complete list, but alone or in combination, they emerge as most significant factors to small business failures. One generalisation is valid here : the success or failure of any small business depends basically on one person, the owner-manager and their ability to manage. They generally face problem by improving their managerial skill. Therefore, final determination for starting a business venture depends upon the availability of managerial talent.

CHAPTER FIVE

FINANCIAL MANAGEMENT : ITS ROLE IN SMALL BUSINESS

Financial Management – its importance in business

Financial management is the conscious effort to formulate long-term policies relating to major aspects of financing, investment and growth decisions with a view to accomplishing the objectives of the firm. The strategic decisions about the different finance functions, which go far beyond the traditional concept of procurement of funds have to take into consideration, the growth strategies and marketing policies, all of which must ultimately become interacting and interdependent part of the same whole.

The commercial world has been changing with the revolutionary industrial and business developments. To cope with these ever-increasing developments and financial management complexities, the authorities in the field of accounting and finance have introduced different financial management tools. Maximization of profit or 'surplus' is the primary objective of an organisation. This objective can be achieved by increasing the cash inflow or by decreasing the cash outflow. In practice, both reduction in the cost of production and increase in the total turnover are aimed at profit maximisation i.e. the better result of a business unit. Realisation of this objective reflects the efficiency and security of the organisation's investment decision. This leads to an increase in the volume of the ownership.

Therefore, efficient and scientific management of finance in an enterprise is of prime importance for achieving the ultimate goal (Sen, Jain and Bala, 2002). In practice, the matter of production or quality or marketing/sales in the ultimate analysis relates to financial issues.

Financial Management touches on all other business functions (Carsberg and Edey, 1969). Most of the business decisions have financial implications and a single decision will often have consequences with financial implications in several different parts of an organisation. Finance is regarded as the lifeblood of a business enterprise. This is because in the money-oriented economy, finance is one of the basic foundations of all economic activities (Maheshwari, 1994). Hence, efficient management of every business organisation is closely linked with efficient management of its finances. An important function of financial management is the coordination of the various decisions taken within an organisation so that they are mutually consistent, having regard for financial aims and constraints. Financial Management is vital for the success of a business, whether it be small or large. Good financial records must be constantly maintained in business if it is to have effective financial control (Pickle and Abrahamson, 1990).

The development of number of management skills and decision-making techniques facilitated to implement a system of optimum allocation of the firm's resources. As a result, the scope of financial management has also changed. The emphasis shifted from episodic financing to managerial financial problems, from raising funds to efficient and effective use of funds (Pandey, 1995). The modern approach is an analytical way of looking into the financial problems of an organisation. Financial management is considered a vital and an integral part of overall management. To quote Ezra Solomon "In this broader view the central issue of financial policy is the wise use of funds and the central process involved is a rational matching of advantage of potential uses against the cost of alternative potential sources so as to achieve the broad financial goals which an enterprise sets of itself". Thus in modern business organisation, the finance functions are said to influence production, marketing and sales and other functions of the firm. This in consequence, will affect the size, growth, profitability and risk of the firm and ultimately, the value of the firm (Pandey, 1995). To quote Ezra Solomon "... the function of financial management is to review and control decisions to commit or recommit funds to new or ongoing uses. Thus, in addition to raising funds, financial management is directly concerned with production, marketing and other functions with in an enterprise whenever decisions are made about the acquisition or distribution of assets".

For the effective execution of the managerial finance functions, routine functions have to be performed. Some of the routine finance functions are :

(1) supervision of each receipts and payments and safeguarding of cash balances;

(2) taking care of the mechanical details of new outside financing;

(3) record keeping and reporting.

The financial decisions have a great impact on all other business activities. The new approach to financial management may be broadened to include profit-planning function also. The term profit planning refers to the operating decisions in the areas of pricing, costing, volume of output and the firm's selection of product lines. Profit planning is, therefore, a pre-requisite for optimising investment and financing decisions.

Financial control is one of the major thrust areas of management, which deals with the proper utilisation of financial resources in a way that optimises the possibilities of beneficial decisions in terms of sound financial health of the organisation (Rao and Pramanik, 1996). The emphasis of Financial Control, therefore, lies on effective decision-making by the managers whereby it advocates the application and understanding of organisational behaviour, techniques and theories of behavioural sciences in the area of financial management with a view to evolving the most pragmatic solutions of the financial problems in totality.

Therefore, Financial management has become an integral part of general management function. In the process it considers various aspects of management accounting in order to determine a number of policies, pertaining to credit, inflow and outflow of funds, financial analysis, inventory control, receivable management, payable management, budgetary control, working capital management, etc. with an aim to draw a beneficial plan of the whole capital structure of the organisation. These may facilitate the process of appraisal of the financial performance of the organisation (Rao and Pramanik, 1996).

Financial management, in today's organisation put stress on the preparation of performance standards, measurement of financial transactions through proper record-keeping, evaluation of actual performance and designing of several intervention strategies of management – action for corrective action. So financial management in modern organisation should not only be conversant about the application of management functions but also needs the continuous flow of information in a systematic way, both as input and feed-back, which produces opportunities of confront uncertainties of both external and internal environment of the organisation (Rao and Pramanik, 1996).

Managing finance is no longer that simple as it used to be in the decades goneby. Political and economic conditions have changed so vastly and have become so complicated all over the world that finance has to be handled with variety of strategies and methods to achieve the desired results.

Commercial history is replete with examples where firms have been liquidated not because the technology was obsolete but because there was a complete mismanagement of financial affairs (Rao, 1999). Thus, it is clear that just as man and machine are to be managed properly, finance has also to be well managed.

It will be useful here to quote Peter Drucker "there are the costs of today and costs of tomorrow. I know of no business today which operates at such a rate of return that it can meet the costs of tomorrow. With today's rate of inflation, businesses are not making profit but only destroying capital. One of the primary tasks of management is to reduce the costs of tomorrow and extract the maximum possible out of available capital".

Superficially, it is the job of an owner-manager of a business of having enough money to meet merchandise bills and payrolls and the like, as they become due in time. Fundamentally, it is the job of establishing and following such sound financial policies that the ability to meet obligations promptly will follow as a logical consequence. Many concerns have more than ample capital for their needs but this capital may be so unintelligently used as a result of unsound financial policy that they invite failure. If sound financial management policies are followed, sound financial condition would result.

Organisations with better management skills in that condition are better prepared to withstand economic storms or other unexpected misfortunes. Since in a free market economy only the fittest survive, ordinary business prudence requires that sound financial control be attained and consistently maintained.

Commenting on sound financial management policy by Holtzman and Lewis says that – A management (owner-manager) which understand and works in accordance with the following basic principles will find itself following sound financial policy :

I. An organisation's investment in not 'fixed assets should be in proper proportion to its tangible net worth (Tangible net worth is the amount of capital the owners have in the business exclusive of intangible assets such as goodwill, franchises and similar items).

II. Net working capital should be in proper position to sales.

III. Inventories should be maintained at a figure less than the net-working capital.

These principles of financial management are treated as fundamental as the law of gravity, they apply to all business concerns regardless of size.

Financial management is the conscious effort to formulate long-term policies relating to major aspects of financing investment and growth decisions with a view to accomplishing the objectives of the firm. The strategic decisions about the different finance functions, which go far beyond the traditional concept of procurement of funds have to take into consideration, the growth strategies and marketing policies, all of which must ultimately become interacting and interdependent part of the same whole.

The commercial world has been changing with the revolutionary industrial and business developments. To cope with these ever-increasing developments and the field of accounting and finance have introduced different financial management tools. Maximization of profit or 'surplus' is the primary objective of an organisation. This objective can be achieved by increasing the cash inflow or by decreasing the cash outflow. In practice, both reduction in the cost of production and increase in the total turnover are aimed at profit maximisation i.e. the better result of a business unit. Realisation of this objective reflects the efficiency and security of the organisation's investment decision. This leads to an increase in the volume of the ownership. Therefore, efficient and scientific management of finance in an enterprise is of prime importance for achieving the ultimate goal (Sen, Jain and Bala, 2002). In practice, the matter of production on quality or marketing/sales in the ultimate analysis relates to financial issues.

The paramount importance of finance in a business enterprise has lead to the development of the discipline of Financial Management. Initially it was considered to be an integral part of Financial Accounting. But during the last century, due to development of tools and techniques of Financial Management, it has come to be regarded as a separate branch of accounting. Financial Management is today considered to be different from financial accounting, cost accounting and even management accounting, though Financial Management is closely related to and to a great extent dependent upon, all these facets of accounting (Chatterjee, 1999).

Financial Management has three broad elements, namely Planning, Organisation and Control.

Planning	**Organisation**	**Control**
* Ascertainment of financial needs * Determination of sources of finance/ funds	* Procurement of funds * Allocation of funds	* Monitoring of funds (through 'financial discipline with regard to funds utilisation)

It shows that, accounting in a business organisation is by and large a service function – a staff function in management terminology. But Financial Management is at least one area, which represents more a line function than a staff function.

Financial Management in Small Business

Financial Management is vital for the success of a business whether small or large. Good financial records must be constantly maintained in business if it is to have effective financial control (Pickle and Abrahamson, 1990). Sound record keeping and analysis can generally increase the possibility of solving many unseen problems early and easily. To prevent, their units from spinning 'out of financial control', a small business owner/manager "should start with good financial control system right up front so there is constant knowledge about what is going on" (Peters and

Waterman, 1994). "Without this ongoing control, we would not be able to spot profitability of concerns or opportunities" says William McBride.

Many small business units would prefer to avoid the subject of financial management. No matter how small the business is, proper financial management is critical to its success. It is essential that the owner/manager become involved in this aspect of the business and understand the basic concepts of financial management. Although accountants may provide monthly statements and some advice but the owner/manager him/herself must understand the financial implication of the accounting information in order to plan the future of the business. Many small business failures could have been prevented if the owner had understood their financial statements and know how to use them for decision making; (Kuchl and Lambing 1994).

Small Business with only one major decision-maker are in a unique position as only at this size can a firm manage without having to communicate business information to others. To match the present pace of change in the economy and maintain a competitive edge, the owner/managers of small business units must know personally in correct form the present position of his/her business. So, for small business enterprises to flourish, more sophisticated accounting tools can not be a luxury (Soral and Jain, 1994). As Waterman recommends that small business owners/ managers should "look at this kind of information as a proactive management tool, not merely as historical information". One classic study by Potts (1992) on Financial management and control techniques in small business concludes that "the clearest and most startling distinction between successful and discontinued small business lies in their approach to the use which can be made of accounting information".

In the literature, it is generally agreed that the financial control system exists to ensure that economic resources of the enterprise are used effectively and efficiently in the pursuit of agreed objectives. It is an information system which has a structure of, possibly expense centres, product centres, profit centres or investment centres and a process or set of procedures which govern the planning and control of resources (Roy and Hutchinson 1983).

Literature on the financial management of small business suggests that, there is a considerable number of reasons for believing that the financial management of small business units should be qualitatively as well as quantitatively different from a large organisation. There are various institutional differences such as regulatory influences, sources and types of finance and forms of financial assistance. In addition, quite distinctive inherent characteristics of small enterprises are likely to lead to differences [Levin and Travis (1987) and Petty and Bygrave (1993)] as follows :

- In large enterprises there is frequently separation between management and ownership, whereas small enterprises are more likely to operate as extension of their owner-manager.
- Small businesses may be faced with fewer investment and financing options.
- Small business units often suffer form "resource poverty" particularly of a financial nature.
- Small business units are generally more likely to experience problems associated with the consequences of growth, such as liquidity pressure.
- Small business units 'financial management is inevitably more dependent on the ability of a single-individual or a small number of individuals than is the case in large enterprises.
- The absence of well-formed market for ownership stakes in small enterprises is likely to impact on their financial management.

Therefore, it appears that there are a number of distinguishable characteristics of small enterprise, which are not considered in the maxims of modern finance theory. Owner-managers may lack diversification in financial investments because a large proportion of their wealth is tied up in the firm and because of the high cost of out-side funds. And also due to the total involvement of owner-manager in the management and operating activities of the firm.

In most researches concerning small business financial management strategies, it is assumed that the small business owner-manager bases decisions on a strategy aimed at increasing wealth as much as possible. But this assumption may not hold good (LeCornu, et. al. 1996). There may in fact be substantial differences which are not adequately captured by the normative goal of wealth maximization of owners and which therefore justify a modified financial objective function.

One of the characteristics of a small business is that, they generally lack a management team. There is an owner-manager and there are worker-employees. The owner typically experiences all the management functions. So the role of an owner-manger, which is best known as a decision-maker on matters relating to finance, is very significant. S/he is responsible not only for the procurement and distribution of funds but also for the determination of financial policy of a business organisation within the framework of the fiscal policy.

The finance function primarily includes the selection of projects for investment, identification of the probable sources of funds with an eye on maximum return at minimum cost, determination of how to proceed with the funds for investing in the project and how to spend cash efficiently bringing desired results in favour of the owner. The owner-manager then determines the requirements and sources of working capital. It also includes the checking and controlling of financial activities in the enterprise with the help of different strategic tools. As a monetary interpreter of different activities, the tools of financial management analyses the efficiency of different sections, the performance of different personnel and the utilization of capacity and then report for definite action.

The new developments in economic and financial management theories, appear to have been based on the assumption that the relevant unit of analysis is a large, publicly quoted firm which has ready access to external capital market for equity and debt finance. It is normally assumed that the firm's shares are frequently traded .... And that the capital market is efficient in processing this information and pricing the firm stock (Keasey and Watson, 1993). Few if any of these features are in fact characteristic of the small business sector and therefore, the financial models and tools will need to be greatly modified if they are to be of any real relevance in increasing our understanding of this sector of the economy.

Information Economics for Small Business

Modern era is termed as information age. Individuals, groups, formal or informal organisation etc. produce effective behaviour, if the respective entities can process the information, efficiently (Rao and Pramanik, 1996). Information processing is, therefore, an integral part of any organisation. It is relevant to explore the potentialities of the organisations to process the information. So, ability to process the acquired information of the organisation (formal/informal) determines its extent to exploit opportunities. These opportunities are produced because of the obsolescence of existing knowledge (Rao and Pramanik, 1996).

'Information', and need to optimise 'information processing ability' exist so long as opportunities remain and become a part of uncertain environmental contingencies. Modern organisations (small/large), therefore, strive to enhance respective information processing abilities.

Generally information is identified from the raw data. Data is the subjective or objective recording of any of the trail or qualities of any event or phenomenon which stimulates attention. Specifically, facts, figures, observations, etc. comes under the category of data. These are, therefore, the prime sources of opportunities. It is the information which increases the probability of utilisation of the data by imparting operational classification and cognitive interpretation of the same through a process of metamorphosis which is, in other way, known as decision-making (Sengupta and Kumar, 1996). Through, decision-making, new information is always produced, having higher utility values than the raw data. Information, precisely then, is that part of the classified and interpreted data which definitely brings productive utilisation of the prime data set through cognitive process of decision-making. Here, the role of the man (owner manager) is vital because, the individual not only produces effective information by minimising the errors but also increases his accessibility to information. The individual (owner manager of a small business) alone opts to effective decisions through the application of individual information processing ability, which is very important in proper decision making.

The management of the modern organisation (small or large) needs the steady flow of information in the context of rapidly changing scenario of the environment, affecting the size and functions of the respective organisations in relation to time. It appears that organisation now a days perceive the utility of information in the presence of increasing complexities of decision-making and management control.

Therefore, the target of good and vital information system, is to incite and develop a process of decision-making in a most productive way within the organisation so that it can exploit opportunities, arising out of uncertain contingencies of the environment by minimising the gap between ultimate and actual information through a study flow of the same in a way which fulfills the twin goals i.e. profit maximisation in the short-run and social co-ordination in the long prospective (Rao and Pramanik, 1996).

In this sense, information system generally expands its functional domains to ensure a continuous flow of information from within and outside the organisation, which, if absent, may produce functional catastrophe to the organisation, jeopardising its survival.

To perform its role in an organisation effectively, information has to be perceived to possess a number of characteristics – it has to be seen as credible, reliable, relevant and timely. However, many of the information produced in the course of economic activity do not possess these characteristics. Even information produced explicitly for monitoring purposes may be seriously deficient in terms of one or more of the desired attributes. This is largely because information is an economic good that is often asymmetrically distributed, costly to produce, verify and analysis and which may be used in ways which are not perceived to be in the interest, of the party which possess the information and/or has a responsibility to disclose it (Keasey and Watson, 1993).

Information can be classified into two : (a) Formal

(b) Informal.

Formal information is that which is regularly gathered and disseminated within the organisation to help the management in decision making. Informal information is all the other knowledge acquired by personnel which enables them to do their job effectively but of which there is no written evidence. In a big organisation the formal information will be very extensive in order that the different decision-makers can be kept in the picture. In a very small business organisation with one-decision maker, generally information are kept in informal way i.e. economic record, are not kept in black and white.

But, the small business owner-manager is perhaps in a better position to acquire most of the information and can identify the cost of information.

Some of the specific causes which demand the development of systematic information flow in an organisation are :

(a) Proper planning and control of the organisation through informed decision making.

(b) Proper manpower planning and management.

(c) Product development and cost control.

(d) Proper financial administration.

(e) Proper production management.

(f) Wage and salary administration.

(g) Establishment of systematic management control.

(h) Fulfillment of legal, political and economic requirements.

Therefore, an organisation (small or large) can not ignore the importance of information more particularly financial information, because effective functioning, in terms of good financial health, requires the efficient utilisation of the information with respect of time, cost and purpose. Thus, an efficient organisation is one, which can use information by keeping a balance among above dimensions. To this end, information to the organisation resembles the "flow of blood in a biological system, having a network of nerves and veins".

Small Business unit are generally owned and controlled by a single individual and limited liability did not exist, the owner-manager would have every incentive to apply the correct, utility maximizing decisions. This is because, he or she would personally bear all the costs associated with any mistakes and also be the sole beneficiary of any increase in the value of wealth. In the context of small business owned by single individual (owner – manager), information (financial in nature) serves two main purposes. First at the initial stage it leads to the reduction of uncertainty (adverse selection) and second, after enter into business, information (financial in nature) can reduce moral hazard and uncertainties. Therefore, financial information can lead to better informed decisions since it helps the decision-maker (owner-manager) and improve action choices.

Small Business organisation engaged in economic activity generates a vast amount of potentially useful information. In order to determine the extent of the information available to the small business owner-manager, it is necessary not only to document business records but also to determine what the owner-manager know about their own business irrespective of whether or not it is formally recorded.

Accounting as an Information System

In the literature, it is generally agreed that the financial control system exists to ensure that the economic resources of the enterprise are used effectively in the pursuit of agreed objectives. It is an information system, which has a structure or set of procedures which govern the planning and control of resources. To keep in touch with financial condition on a day-to-day basis the owner-manager of a small business requires accounting information that is accurate, properly organised and continually upto date. A good accounting system must be comprehensive enough to satisfy the purpose of financial control. So there is a close relationship between good accounting and business success. Financial decision based upon inadequate, unreliable or confusing accounting information often lead to financial disaster.

In the year 1970, the AICPA of the USA defined accounting with reference to the concept of 'Information' :

'Accounting is a service activity. Its function is to provide quantitative information primarily financial in nature about economic activities that is intended to be useful in making economic decisions'. The modern accounting therefore, is not merely concerned with the record-keeping but also is concerned with a whole range of activities involving :

(a) Planning (b) Control (c) Decision making (d) Problem solving (e) Performance measurement and evaluation (f) Co-ordinating and directing (g) Auditing (h) Tax determination and Planning. (i) Cost accounting (j) Management Accounting. Therefore, today's accounting focuses on the ultimate needs of those who use accounting information, whether these users are insiders or outsiders.

Many research studies and literature on financial management has proved that there is a close relationship between good accounting practices and business success. To keep in touch with financial conditions on a day-to-day basis requires accounting information that is accurate, properly organised and continually upto data. A good accounting system must be comprehensive enough to satisfy the purpose of financial control (Stegall, et. al. 1994). Entrepreneurs often blame their failures on low sales revenues, the wrong mix of inventory, high operation

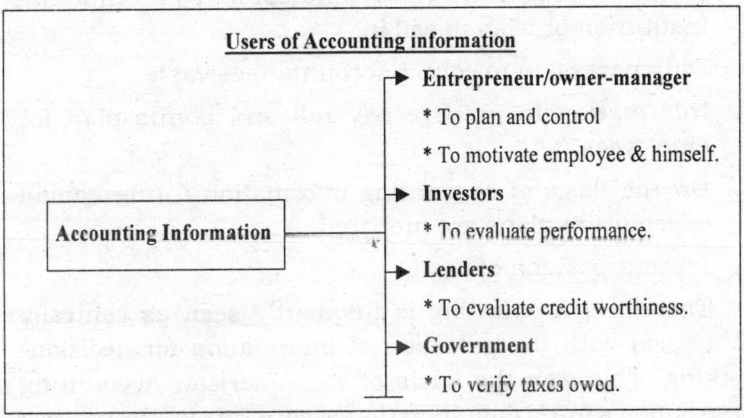

expenses, insufficient cash, or too much money tied up in fixed assets. Yet, with a well-designed accounting system, an entrepreneur can spot these problems early and head them off. Accounting figures are the compass readings that show the pilot of the shop of business the speed and direction in which the firm is travelling (Harmon, 1979).

Accounting has been described succinctly and accurately as "the measurement and communication of financial and economic data'. The accounting is the major channel through which quantitative information flows to management (Lynch and Williamson, 1994). Accounting records have always been important because they provide the owner-manager with a sense of direction and tools for control. (Harmon, 1979). Accounting Records is even more important today. It provides the owner-manager with the following information of the business :

1. A system to measure profitability and performance.
2. Data upon which to base forecasts.
3. Information for Government reports/taxes and licenses.
4. Evidence that a firm has paid its dues (bills) and other data used to disprove fraud or claims against the business.
5. Financial data necessary to show value of the firm, if the owner-manager want to take loan from financial institution or wish to sell it.
6. Data necessary to collect accounts receivable.
7. Information to prepare pay roll and bonus plan for employees.
8. On the basis of accounting information future capital expenditure plans are prepared.
9. Present position of cash.

Therefore, Accounting is frequently seen as centrally concerned with the provision of information for decision-making. This was the basis of the American Accounting Association's (AAA) definition that accounting is "the process of identifying, measuring and communicating economic information to permit informed judgements and decision by users of the information". Accounting information are seen as objective truth about the enterprise and are carefully gathered so that they are comprehensive, valid and reliable. They are selected on the basis of their relevance to particular decision, are processed through the application of universally established accounting methods/techniques/rules and presented to decision-maker as the necessary information from which decision will flow. Accounting information is rational because it deals with facts rather than opinions, prejudices or guesses.

A business organisation is regarded as an open system which has a dynamic interplay with its environment from which it draws resources and to which it consigns its products and services. (Das, Sinha, et. al. 1999).

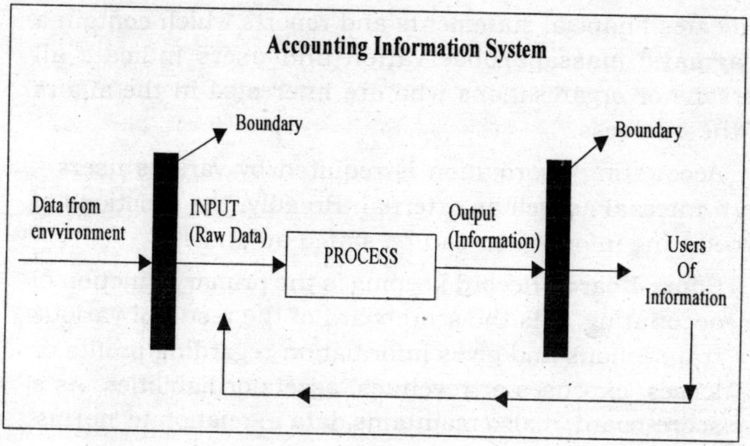

Accounting comprises a series of activities which are inter-linked. They with observing, collecting, recording, analysing and finally communicating the observed information to its users. Accounting system has three distinct activities viz. (1) Inputs (2) Processing of inputs and (3) Outputs.

Business transaction take place in the regular business activities collected and recorded are called raw data or accounting inputs. These accounting inputs are then processed through classifying, summarising, analysing and interpreting by using different techniques of accounting. This work on the accounting inputs is known as accounting process. These processed data are stored until they are needed.

The processed data/inputs known as accounting output which become information, is then communicated to the users and decision-makers. As we considered accounting as an information system, it establishes a link among the sources of information, a channel of communication and a set of receivers. Here the source of information means the books of accounts which are the repository of accounting data to be needed by different users, channel of information indicates financial statements and reports which contain a pragmatic massage/observation and users indicate all persons or organisations who are interested in the affairs of the business.

Accounting information is required by various users – both internal as well as external. Broadly, the functions of accounting information can be stated as under :

- **Score-Board :** Record keeping is the primary function of accounting. It is the scoreboard of the result of various transactions and gives information regarding profits or losses, expenses or revenues, assets or liabilities. As a score-board, it also maintains data in relation to 'norms' or 'predetermined standards' and thereby enables a comparison of actual data with standards or judge the health of an enterprise.
- **Store-house of accounting and other economic information :** Accounting information in an enterprise records all the information in monetary terms and the information can be made use of various purposes.
- **Attention direction :** Accounting information is needed by the decision makers to focus on deviations from the planned objectives or the budget or standards and to take correct actions.
- **Problem solving :** Accounting provides information for problem solving. Management is very often confronted with a number of problems and has to take decisions to solve these problems. Accounting information enables the manager to quantify different alternative solutions to the problem with the relative merits and demerits of each alternatives.

The administrative function of management develops from its economic function. The main function of management in an organisation is to plan, organise and control. Each of these activities encompasses a large number of complex and interrelated day-to-day actions. In a going concern, these activities are carried on simultaneously. These three (planning, organising and controlling) administrative activities have one thing in common. Each requires that decisions be made. What ever their form or impact, all decisions have two characteristics in common :

(i) They involve choosing among available alternatives.

(ii) They culminate in action from which certain consequence flow.

Because a decision involves choosing, it follows that some rational activity has preceded it. The decision maker (i.e. management/owner-manager in small business) chooses what he perceives to be the greatest 'good' in a given situation. Here lies the importance of accounting information as accounting has been described succinctly and accurately on "the measurement and communication of financial and economic data". The accounting is the major channel through which quantitative information flows to management. Through accounting information, the owner-manager/management first decide what is relevant and what is irrelevant and rank the relevant according to its degree of importance to management.

Thus it is, clear that accounting is more than 'reporter' or information collector, but it interpret the acquired information or accounting data's as a 'editor' (Lynch and Williamson, 1994). In this way, accounting information is able to influence the decision-makers toward achieving better results.

It may be concluded that accounting as an information system is very crucial for several disciplines which supplement the business operation (Sikidar and Nath, 2002).

The Basic Financial Records for a Small Business

A business must record every financial transaction. Records have always been important because they provide the manufacturer / merchant with a sense of direction and tools for control. The financial records of a business begin with the documents that indicate the business transactions as they take place, which includes such things as sales receipts, cash received, purchase orders, invoices, monthly statements from supplies etc. Thus, every financial transaction regardless of how informal, should produce some sort of written record.

The data to record include :

- Sales orders received
- Invoices issued by the business for sales
- Purchase orders placed by the business
- Invoices received by the business for purchases
- Cash receipts
- Cash expenditure
- Account receivable / payable

Not all of these records apply to all businesses. For example, some service firms do not carry inventory and maintains no inventory records. Similarly, not all business extends credit to customers; therefore, an accounts receivable record would not be needed. A general record keeping system for a small business should include at least the following accounting records for financial decision making.

1. **Accounts Receivable :** Records of receivables are vital not only to decisions on credit extension but also to accurate billing and to maintenance of good customer relations. Analysis of these records reveals the degree of effectiveness of the firm's / business credit and collection policies.

2. **Accounts Payable** : Records of liabilities shows what the business / firm owes, facilitate the taking of cash discounts and allow payments to be made when due.
3. **Inventory Records** : Adequate records are essential to the control and security of inventory items. In addition, they supply information to the business in purchasing, maintenance if adequate stock level and computation of turnover ratios.
4. **Cash Records** : Carefully maintained records showing all receipts and disbursements are necessary to safeguard cash. They yield a knowledge of cash flow and balances on hand in a particular point of time, such information is essential for the proper timing of loans and for assurance of cash to pay obligations.
5. **Other Records** : Among other accounting records which are vital to the efficient operation of the small business are the payroll records which show the total payments to employees; records covering the firm's investments outside its business, computation of cost of sales / cost of production and services, Drawing / withdraws by the owner manager for personal use, etc.

These data will enable the business to prepare :

- Production schedules
- Purchasing requirements
- Profitability and efficiency
- Liquidity and solvency
- Stock level of raw materials, work in progress and finished goods.
- Age of debtors
- Age of creditors
- Cost of production and proper pricing.

All the financial information of a business is derived from the book-keeping systems. While some of the techniques of book-keeping may appear more appropriate for larger business, they will also help very small business as well. Whatever record-keeping system the small business owner –manager chooses, it should follow the following criteria :

- **Simple to use** : Unless a record-keeping systems is simple to use, the owner, who usually is pressed for time, probably will disregard it.
- **Easy to understand** : The system must be so clear that everyone who uses it can understand the information it presents.
- **Reliable** : The record-keeping system adopted by the small business, must perform the functions it is designed to perform and measure the aspects of the business it is needed to measure.
- **Accurate :** Financial Management can be only as accurate as the records and reports used. Faulty information leads to faulty managerial decisions.
- **Consistent** : The system must parallel the operation of the business and should reflect the firm's financial status consistently over time.
- **Designed to provide timely information** : To make sound day –to-day managerial and financial decisions, the owner-manager of a small business requires up-to-date information.

Just as a homebuilder first lay the foundation, do the framing, put up the walls and then do the finish work. A small business owner-manager also must proceeds steep-by-steep. In the early stage of a business, the most cost-effective method of book-keeping is to keep the books manually. The actual frame of records can be linked to General Records. They are the underlying materials without which there could be no walls. In the same way, General Records of every business transactions are the basis (source of information) for forming Financial statements.

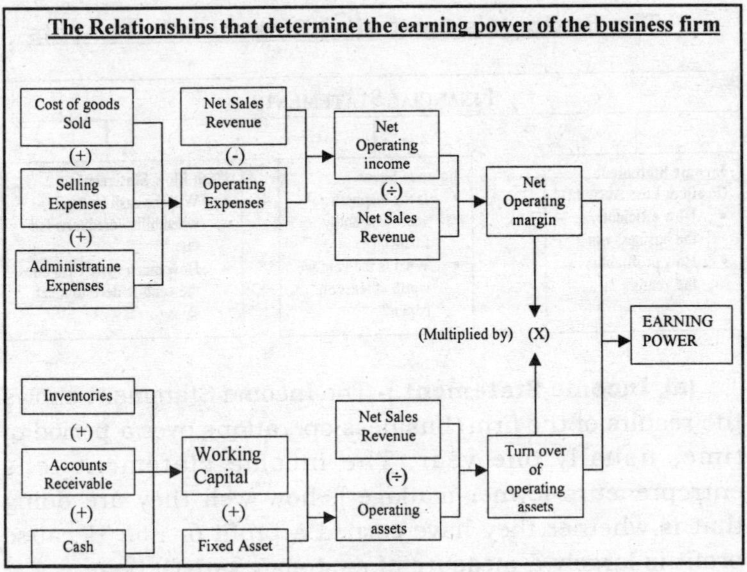

[*Source* : Stegall, Steinmetz and Khine (1994)]

Accounting records are not only the books used to record the business transactions but it also includes all the invoices both issued and received by the business. The business should file its records in an orderly manner, including purchase invoices and sales invoices, as this will assist in keeping accurate accounting records and ready reference.

Typical Financial Statements

The preparation of Financial Statements is made possible by the existence of accurate and thorough accounting records. Three most important financial statements are :

a) The Income Statement

b) The Balance Sheet.

c) The Cash Flow Statement.

The Business's most vital Financial Statements

FINANCIAL STATEMENTS

Income Statement
(Profit & Loss Account)
- How efficiently is the business run ?
- How profitable is the venture ?

Balance Sheet
- Is the business venture soundly financed ?
- What is the vent we worth at least on paper ?

Cash Flow Statement
- Will the cash be there when bills / creditons fall due ?
- How much more cash does the venture need to meet sales forecasts ?

(a) Income Statement :- The Income Statement shows the results of the firm/business operations over a period of time, usually one year. The income statement tells entrepreneurs (owner-manager), how well they are doing that is whether they have earned a profit or not. Because profit is largely a measure of customer satisfaction.

In its simplest form, an income statement looks like as follows :

Income Statement of a Service Unit
(Computer Programmer (DTP Operator) for one year)

	Sales revenues	Rs. 24,000.00
Less :	Operating expenses	Rs. 18,000.00
Therefore,	Operating Profit	Rs. 6,000.00

From the above example, it can be observed that profit is what remains after operation expenses have been deducted from sales revenues; profit, then, is the net effect of two opposing flows of money.

- Money flowing into the business/firm from sales made to customers, either for cash or on credit (generally called sales revenues)
- Money flowing out of the business from costs earned in connection with making those sales (generally called operating expenses).

The example cited above is typical only for service industry/business; which do not sell products that customers can touch and see. For industry groups that do – retailing, wholesaling and manufacturing – the income statement also include an item called cost of goods sold, as following example:

Income Statement of a Retailer/Whole seller/ Manufacturer

	Sales Revenues	Rs. 24,000.00
Less.	Cost of goods sold	Rs. 15,000.00
	Gross profit	Rs. 9,000.00
Less.	Operating Expenses	Rs. 3,000.00
	Operating Profit	Rs. 6,000.00

For retailers, the cost of goods sold generally represents what they paid to whole-sellers for the products they resold to customers. For wholesalers, it represents what they paid manufacturers for the products, they resold to retailers. And for manufacturers, it represents, for those products sold to customers, the cost of converting raw materials into finished products plus the cost of raw materials.

Income statement or the Trading and Profit and Loss Account describes how the assets have been used to generate profit and how that profit was used. The calculation of profit of a business unit is a matter of "judgement" : in the estimated life of the fixed asset and in the amount of depreciation to write off each year, underlines an important judgement. There are other areas where judgement is exercised in deciding on profit. Judgement is required when a business will know that some of the debtors (account receivable) will not eventually pay up and therefore will not show these debtors in the balance-sheet or will set up a 'provision' in case the debts are not paid. Similarly judgements regarding the quality and quantity of stock must also be made and some old damaged or useless stock might not be shown in the balance sheet or, again, a 'provision' might be set up in case the stock proves unsaleable.

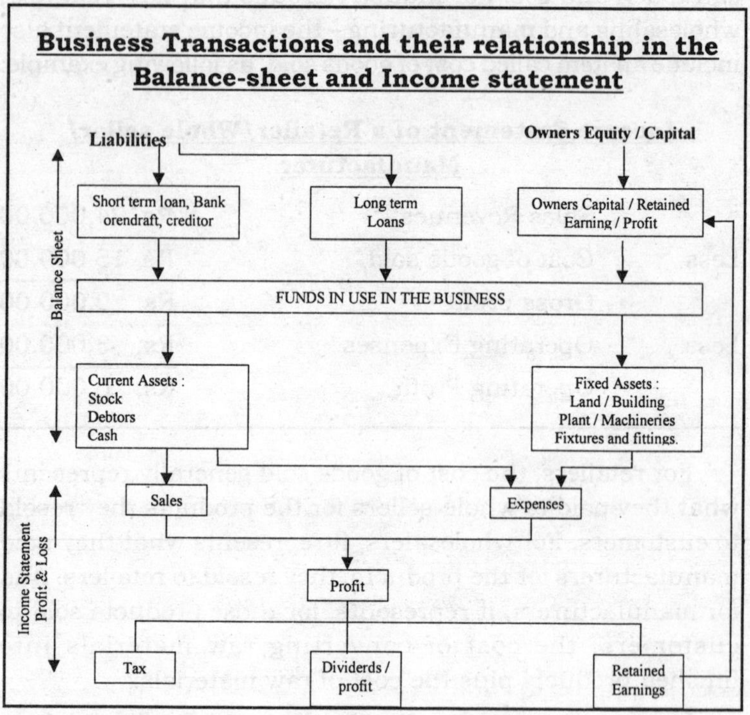

Source : Dewhurst and Burns (1983).

The point is that financial measurement is not exact. Profit is the result of certain judgements that people make and therefore, it is an estimate of the growth of assets through trading, not an exact calculation of it (Dewhurst and Burns, 1983). Certain accounting principles have developed to help accountants in this area of judgement.

(b) The Balance Sheet

Just as the income statement summarises how well a business venture has done over time, the balance sheet summarises its financial health as of a particular point of time. The balance sheet tells entrepreneurs (owner-manager of a small business) :

- What their business venture is worth, at least on paper.
- What they have invested in assets, such as inventories, Land and Building, Plant and Machineries.
- How the assets were financed – that is, where the money came from to buy them.
- Who has what claims against the assets.

The balance sheet is built on the fundamental accounting equation :

Assets = Liabilities + Capital.

Any increase or decrease on one side of the equation must be effect by an equal increase or decrease on the other side; hence the name balance sheet.

Structure of Accounting system

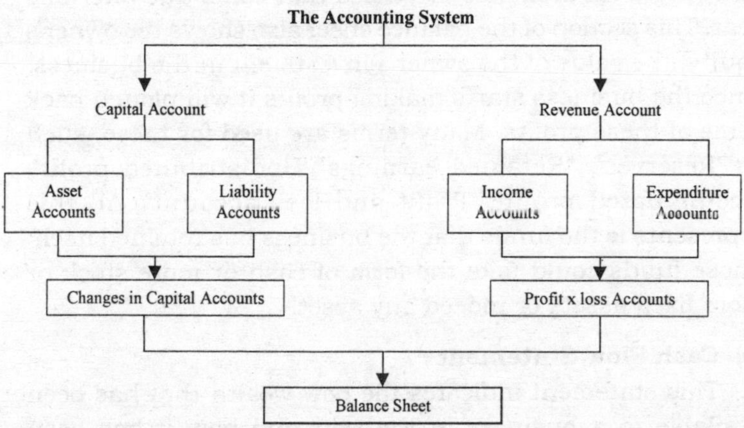

The first section of the balance sheet lists the firm's assets and shows the total value of everything the business owns. Current assets consist of cash and items to be converted into cash with in one year, such as account receivable and inventory and fixed assets are those acquired for long-term use in the business. Intangible assets include items that, although valuable, do not have tangible value, such as goodwill, copyrights trade marks, and patents – also treated as an asset in a business.

Balance Sheet as on 1/1/2003

Assets	Rs.	Liabilities	Rs.
Cash/Bank	40,000.00	Bank loan	30,000.00
Closing Stock	20,000.00	Capital (owners equity)	30,000.00
Debtors	5,000.00	Creditor	5,000.00
	65,000.00		65,000.00

The second section shows the business's liabilities – the creditor's claims against the business assets. Current liabilities are those debts that must be paid with in one year and long term liabilities are those that come due after one year. This section of the balance sheet also shows the owner's equity, the value of the owner's investment in the business. Once the business starts making profits it will plough back some of these profits. Many terms are used for these, such as 'Reserves', "Retained earnings' 'Undistributed profit', 'accumulated profit', 'Profit and loss account'. All this represents is the funds that the business has retained itself. Those funds could take the form of cash or more stock or more fixed assets or indeed any asset.

(c) Cash Flow Statement

This statement indicates the new wealth that has been available to a business in the year and how it has been invested in the business. They can be constructed to highlight changes in the firm's/business's cash position. They emphasize different aspects of management of finance.

To prepare the statement, the balance sheets and the income statements summarising the present year's operations must be assembled. Then the sources of funds – net income, borrowed funds, owner's contributions, etc. are listed. Next the uses of these funds are listed : plant and equipment purchases, profit distributed, repayment of debt and so on.

Cash Flow Statement is vital in forward planning and it is obligatory for all business to publish a cash flow statement showing the source of funds and their use (FRS 1).

The main source of Funds	**Uses or application of funds**
*Capital introduced by owner	*Owner's withdrawals.
*Loans to business	*Loan repayments.
*Sale of assets	*Purchase of assets.
*Income from operation	*Losses from operation.
	*Payments to tax authorities.

The difference between the total sources and the total uses is the increase or decrease in working capital. Surplus or shortfalls are noted in the reconciliation of opening and closing balance. By investigating the changes in the firm's working capital and the reasons for them, owners-managers of small businesses can create a more practical financial plan of action for the future of the enterprise. They can also help small business managers map the firms/business's financial future and actively plan for profit. Cash flow statements are now required in financial reports because success depends on maximising the flow of cash throughout the year.

Circular flow of funds showing sources and applications of funds/cash.

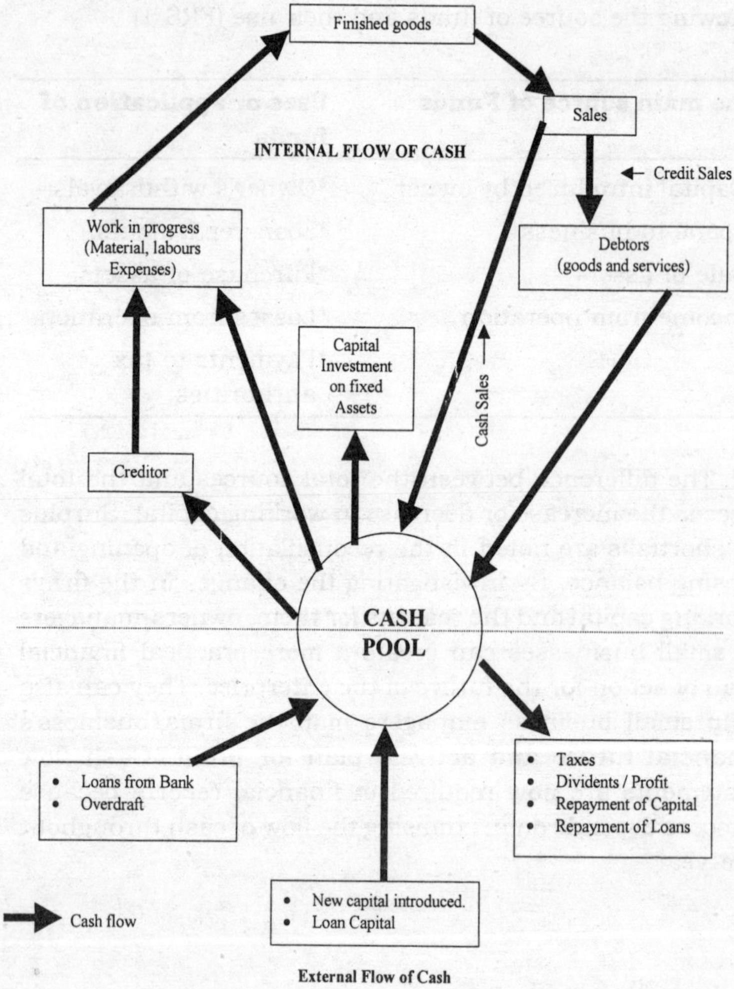

Source : Modern Business Administration (1994).

Mere preparation of these statements, i.e. (a) Profit and Loss a/c (b) Balance sheet and (c) Cash flow statement, is not enough; owner-manager must understand and use the information contained in them. These data are critical to the success and the ultimate survival of the business.

Tools of Financial Management

In performing the responsibilities and duties more effectively and efficiently, the owner-manager of a small business may take the assistance of various techniques of financial management. Amongst the various techniques of financial management, most commonly used techniques are analysis of financial statements, Ratio Analysis, Cash Budgeting, Cost-volume Profit analysis and Capital Budgeting.

(i) Income Statements

Financial analysis comprises the various financial statement items according to some logical criteria. This statement comprises the balance sheet and the profit and loss Account or income statement. This two statements are the very important means by which a business firm can be viewed in its entirely as they represents the whole firm's activities/performance from different aspects.

Financial Analysis is required by outside suppliers of capital, creditors and investors and also by the firm itself. The type of analysis varies according to the specific interest of a party. A trade creditor is interested in the liquidity of the firm. An Investor is mainly with its present and expected future earnings and the stability of these earnings in the long run. And the internal management is interested in showing the outside creditors and investor or financiers a better financial position and sound operating ability of the firm through the analysis of the financial statements. Moreover, for internal control it is a must at regular intervals (Sen, Jain and Bala, 2002).

(ii) Cash Budget/Budgeting

Budget is nothing but a financial plan of the enterprise

over a short and a long period of time. A cash budget is the forecast of future cash receipts and cash disbursements over various intervals of time. It reveals to the management, the timing and amount of expected cash flows and outflows over the period under study. With its information, an owner-manager is better equipped to determine the future cash needs of the business, plan for the financing of these needs and exercise control over the cash and liquidity of the firm.

The preparation of cash budget involves the following steps : (monthly cash budget)

1. Estimate monthly receipts assuming no additional financing;
2. Estimate monthly expenditures;
3. Comparison between the monthly receipts and expenditures assuming no additional financing.
4. Estimating cash balances to be available at the month assuming no additional financing.
5. Forecasting the fluctuations in cash inflows and outflows and determination of the extent of a 'cash-cushion' to be built up for meeting such derivations.

(iii) Cost-Volume-Profit (CVP) Analysis

CVP analysis is a Financial Management tool, which can be very effectively used in planning and control activities of business enterprise. It provides the measuring devices and needs only the master's touch to produce the right mixture (Sen, Jain and Bala, 2002).

In planning, CVP Analysis can be used to determine whether efforts would be better directed towards the reduction of fixed and variable costs. It can be used to arrive at decisions involving the interaction of selling prices and sales volume. It provides the only sound basis for predicting profits and can point out where sales efforts should be directed/emphasised. Therefore, it is a means of evaluating sales performance.

As a control device, CVP analysis can be used to detect

the insidious upward creep of costs that might otherwise, go unnoticed. It reveals whether actual performances were as profitable as they should have been (Sen, et. al. 2002). In analysing performances, it is far superior to percentage comparisons that mislead as often as they inform. The tool of cost-volume-profit Analysis, which is popularly known as break-even analysis, reflects, the whole position usually with the help of a break-even-chart.

The break-even point found out through the analysis gives a situation, below which point production or turnover is undesirable. Basing on this analysis, different costs can be adjusted and efforts may be generated for striking a balance between the cost, volume and profit of the business. Mathematical calculation of the break-even point is done with the help of the following formula :

Break-Even Point (volume in units)

$$BEP = \frac{\text{Total fixed costs (F)}}{\text{Selling price per unit (P)} - \text{Variable cost per unit (V)}}$$

The Break-Even Point can also be calculated for Break-even Sales Volume (expressed in monetary value) which is F/CMR, where CMR represents 'contribution margin ratio' [=(P-V)/P] or P/V ratio [= DP/DV]

(iv) Ratios Analysis

Financial statements are interpreted (analysised) by calculating certain ratio. Ratios show the relationship between two items. Ratios are the tools with which business can measure performance and are used in the analysis of financial statements because a business owner-manager might be misled by a comparison of money figures alone.

Financial ratios can be used in the determination of policies for future operation of the business in two ways. First, business owners may find if helpful to compare their firm's ratios for the period under scrutiny with similar ratios for the previous periods/years. Such comparison can often help to pinpoint conditions in their business that merit attention.

Second, business owners can compare the ratios for their business with the standard ratios in their industry/ sector of business. Standard ratios are averages of the results achieved by thousands of firms in the same line of business.

There are four main types of ratios that may be used in examining the financial health of a business enterprise :

1. Profitability Ratios, which measure the firms, earnings in relation to sales and investment.
2. Liquidity Ratio, which indicate the firm's ability to pay its bills/dues as they become due.
3. Turnover Ratio, which measures low effectively the firm, uses its resources to general sales or profit.
4. Leverage Ratio, which measure the firm's debt load.

(v) Capital Budgeting

Capital budgeting may be defined as the formal planning of the sources of long-term funds and their allocation among potential long-term uses. This process involves one of the important functions of financial management. Owner-manager of a business has to take a judicious decision on the investment of the available funds in the desirable projects. This decision is most important because, it involves a huge sum of money and its effects will be felt for a long period of time. Another important aspect of the major investment decision is that until such decision is made and implemented many other related decisions cannot be undertaken. Therefore, it shows that, decisions reached through the process of capital budgeting are of extreme importance to the long-term success of a business enterprise.

Capital budgeting involves the generation of investment proposals, the estimate of cash flows for the future capital investment proposals, the evaluation of cash flows and the selection of projects based upon an acceptance criterion. Capital investment decision involves the measuring of investment worth of a proposal. The methods of measuring are :

Computing Financial Ratios Measuring a Business's Financial Health

I PROFITABILITY RATIOS :	**Numerator**	**Denominator**
* Gross Margin Ratio	Gross Margin	Net Sales
* Net Profit Ratio	Net Profit	Net Sales
	or	
	Net Profit	Average tangible net worth
II LIQUIDITY RATIOS :	**Numerator**	**Denominator**
* Current Ratio	Current Assets	Current Liabilities
* Acid-Test Ratio	Current Assets - (Inventories)	Current Liabilities
III TURNOVER RATIO :	**Numerator**	**Denominator**
* Working capital turnover ratio	Net sales	Current Assets – Current Liabilities
* Investment capital turnover ratio	Fixed Assets	Tangible net worth
* Inventory turnover Ratio	Cost of goods sold	Average inventory at cost.
	or	
	Net Sales	Average inventory at retail.
* Receivables turnover Ratio : Average daily credit sales	Net sales on Account	365 days
Average collection period	Average receivable +Notes Receivables.	Average daily credit sales.
IV LEVERAGE RATIOS :	**Numerator**	**Denominator**
* Debt-Equity Ratio	Current liabilities + Fixed liabilities	Tangible Net Worth
* Fixed debt load	Fixed liabilities	Fixed Assets.

1. Payback Period Method
2. Average Rate of Return
3. Discounted cash flow Method :
   (a) Internal Rate of Return (IRR)
   (b) Net Present Value Method (NPV)
   (c) Profitability Index.

1. Payback Method

This method indicates the time to be required to recover the original investment and is usually expressed in terms of years. Payback Period is calculated by using the formula :

$$\text{Payback Period} = \frac{\text{Net cash outlay (NCO)}}{\text{Annual net cash benefits (NCB)}}$$

If this method is used for evaluating a series of competing investment proposals, the project which has the shortest payback period is accepted.

2. Average Rate of Return Method

It is an accounting method and represents the ratio of the average annual profits after taxes to the initial investment. The rate is arrived at by using the following formula :

$$\text{Average Rate of Return} = \frac{\text{Average annual NCB x 100\%}}{\text{Net investment (NCO)}}$$

Where; NCB = Net cash benefit

NCO = Net cash outlay

The project which yields a higher rate of return is normally accepted.

3. Discounted cash flow Method

According to this method, the cash outflow (Net capital investment) and the expected cash inflows of the investment are discounted at an appropriate cost of capital to their present values. The present values can then be analysed to determine the suitability of the project.

The Discounted Cash flow technique includes the following methods :

(a) Internal Rate of Return (IRR)

IRR for an investment proposal is defined as that discounted rate which, when applied to a series of future NCB, (Net cash benefit) marks the present value of NCBs equal to the present value of the NCO (Net cash outlay) necessary to generate them. IRR is then compared to a required rate of return and if it exceeds the required rate the project is accepted.

(b) Net Present Value Method (NPV)

NPV is the present value of net cash benefits discounted at the appropriate cost of capital minus the NCO (Net cash outflow). Under this method, the present value of the expected net cash benefits of an investment is ascertained by discounting at the cost of capital and subtracting from it the net cash outlay of the project. If the NPV is positive, the project is accepted; if negative, it is rejected.

(c) Profitability Index (PI)

This method places all projects on the same comparable basis. If the PI for a given project is greater than 100, the project is accepted. The formula for calculating the Profitability Index (PI) is :

$$PI = \frac{\text{Gross Present Value of NCB x 100\%}}{\text{Present Value of NCO}}$$

Where,

NCB = Net Cash benefit

NCO = Net cash outflow.

Elements of Cost and Price

Many business establishments have difficulty in calculating the cost of their products or services and as a result, let their competitor get the weaknesses and set their price. As mentioned in all the financial management books, profit is the relatively small difference between the two relatively large numbers of sales revenue and expenditure. A small change in any one of those can cause a large change in profit, so getting both pricing and cost right is clearly very important.

Every business units need to charge a price that will cover all the costs and generate a reasonable profit to stay in the business. It is very important to note that, there is little relationship between costing and pricing. The price should be the maximum amount that people will pay for business product or services. The cost on the other hand is the cost of a business of making the product or delivering the services. Costing/Cost Accounting methods of financial management aim to allocate costs between jobs and periods. In addition, however, business objectives should always include attempts to reduce costs and to improve productivity. Keeping the price high and the costs low will therefore, maximise profit for the organisation.

It is therefore, very important to know how to spread the costs. It is easy to see all the different costs that a business incurs, but it is often helpful to divide these up.

- **Direct Cost** are those that can be directly attributed (usually measurable) to the production of a particular product or service. Raw materials are direct costs. Sub-contracting is a direct cost. Deducting the direct costs from the sales revenue for a particular product gives its contribution towards over-heads and profit.
- **Variable Cost** are those that vary in proportion to the level of production. These will include for example, raw materials, direct labour and sub-contract work. However, some over-head costs, such as use of electricity, may also vary with total production. Variable cost are also called as marginal costs.
- **Fixed Costs,** on the other hand, do not vary in the short run and are not dependent on the level of production. This includes, for example, rent, rate, insurance and manager's salary.

- **Indirect Costs** are the opposite of direct costs – those costs that cannot be directly attributed to a specific product. The overheads are indirect, some will vary with the level of production, and some will be fixed. For most small businesses, the overheads can generally be regarded as fixed, at least in the short term.

A manufacturing unit can calculate the cost per item by:

$$\text{Item Cost} = \frac{\text{Overheads}}{\text{Total items}} + \text{Direct cost per item}$$

A service based business unit can calculate the cost of services :

If the service provider involves in business's such as industrial design or software development, etc. then the business will need to know how much to charge per hour, through estimating the total time required. This can be done by :

$$\text{Hourly Rate} = \frac{\text{Over heads}}{\text{Annual Productive hours}}$$

Small business owner-manager, must remember that not all working hours will be productive. Some time will be required for promoting the business, buying supplies, doing the book-keeping work etc. There may be some holidays and should also allow for possible illness.

Some businesses are simply engaged in buying and selling; many of those are particularly retailers, selling an extremely wide range of products. They tend to think about the mark-up required to cover their other overheads. The mark-up is simply the inverse of the Gross Profit margin. Therefore, before establishing a mark-up price, the business need to estimate likely total sales and to know all the overhead expenses/costs. Business margin must still cover all overhead costs, otherwise, the business will not make any profit.

Pricing Strategies

The greatest danger for a business (small/large) is to setting a price for their products/services for the first time is to pitch it too low. On the other hand raising a price in the competitive market is always more difficult than lowering one. Therefore, while selecting a price of products/ services, the owner-manager of a small business can choose any of the following pricing strategies :

- Cost based pricing - total costs are calculated and a mark up is added to give the required profit.
- Skimming - business may change a relatively high price to recover set up costs quickly if the product is good or new. As more competitors enter the market, producer can lower the price.
- Individual - business unit can negotiate prices individually with customers based on how much the proposed buyer are prepared to buy.
- Loss leaders - if the business wish to sell to a particular market then the business organisation might sell one product or services cheaper to gain market entry. And the organisation can balance these losses by selling other products/services at a higher price. This can be risky, as the danger is that everything becomes a loss leader.
- Expected price - what does the customer expected to pay ? If the business organisation are selling a quality product/services, do not underprice. Often the customer expected to pay a lot as the product/services has a certain 'snob' value and this may be diminished if the business is underprice.
- Differential pricing - the organisation can change different segments of market/customers different prices for the same service/products.

It is to be mentioned here that, if the cost of a product/ services of a business and the price change is much higher than the competitors' then the organisation will have to look at ways of reducing costs.

Computing the Cost of sales in various Types of Small Business

1. Trading / Merchandising Establishments :

Merchandise inventory, beginning of period (year)

(+) New purchases during the year.

(-) Merchandise inventory end of the year

(=) Cost of goods sold.

2. Manufacturing Establishments :

Raw materials inventory, beginning of period (year)

(+) Purchases

(-) Raw materials inventory at the end of the year.

(=) Raw materials used.

(+) Direct Labour

(+) Factory over head (indirect labour, machine and plant depreciation, repairs and maintaining)

(+) Work – in – progress – inventory, beginning of the period.

(-) Work – in – progress – inventory, end of the period.

(=) Cost of manufacturing.

(+) Finished goods inventory, beginning of period.

(-) Finished goods inventory, end of the period.

(=) Cost of goods sold.

3. Service Business :

Spare Parts – inventory (beginning of the period).

(-) Purchases

(-) Spare parts – inventory (end of the period).

(=) Cost of parts (on service supplies)

(-) Service labour (labour directly cost to individual customers order)

(-) Cost of merchandise sold, if any.

(=) Cost of sales.

Inventory Management

The management of funds invested in inventory is important because in many cases inventory is the largest single asset, particularly on the current side. Equally important is the fact that inventory is the least liquid current asset; hence errors in management are not readily remedied.

Inventory control is one of the elements of financial management, and carried out successfully can materially increase the profits of the business. It need not be expensive to the small business unit. A small amount spent in setting up and maintaining a system of inventory control may very well disclose hidden losses that would not otherwise be brought to the surface. As it is said that an excessive stock of materials and supplies represents idle working capital – in fact, too much of it means 'dead' capital.

The purpose of controlling inventory is to maintain a stock balance that permits profitable operations with the least cost. The major objectives are as follows :

1. To secure maximum sales by having the goods on hand to meet demand.
2. To protect the inventory from theft, deterioration, rust, decay and destruction.
3. To assure continuous operational flow in manufacturing unit.
4. To minimise the cost of carrying the inventory, including interest on money invested obsolescence, insurance, taxes and cost of warehousing.
5. To provide records of purchase quantities, order dates and other data essential for evaluation of management performance.

Therefore, Inventory (stores) control as a system of keeping track of the merchandise received and merchandise sold – or in even simpler words, the 'ins' and 'outs'.

It is essential that every class of business have some

form of stock book, recording the items coming in and the items going out. Where there are only a few items involved, a notebook page for each item will suffice. But, once the small business unit has discovered the full value of inventory records he will wish to have slightly more elaborate stock books for the permanent history of the business.

There are a number of costs associated with carrying inventory. First, there is the cost of funds invested in inventory and equipment to handle the inventory. Next, there is the cost associated with the space occupied by the inventory, which may include depreciation charges, maintenance charges, rental charge taxes, etc. Then there may certain inventory service costs, such as taxes and insurance, the labour costs of receiving and stocking, inventory record and book-keeping costs, pilferage costs. Finally, there may be the costs associated with the risk of a price decline, the risk of a style changes or other causes of obsolescence.

In considering the cost of excess inventory, it is important to recognise those that will vary with the level of the inventory carried and those, which are fixed at least in the short run (Stock) level. The business unit first of all must determine what quantities are most economical to buy. Closely related to this is the question of safety stocks to absorb unexpected fluctuation in inventory availability or sales. Here the owner-manager of a small business has to weight the cost of being out of stock against the cost of maintaining the safety stock. Another important area of inventory management is the lead time necessary in ordering inventory, that is, the time period involved in ordering and receiving delivery.

Let us start, with a very simple illustration of stock recording process for different sector of small business :

(a) Manufacturer

The stock (inventory) records of a manufacturing business should be as detailed as possible. Generally the manufacturer has there classes of inventory : Raw materials (which may includes component/spare parts or factory supplies); goods in process; and finished goods. As a manufacturer always attempt to determine what quality of raw materials to order and finished goods to stock, they try to seek a balance. Another force advises the manufacturer to stock raw materials heavily and avoid the risk of running out of stock.

One of the earlier systems designed to strike this balance is called the minimum – maximum formula. It computes a medium between minimum stock required and maximum stock usable. A more precise method for achieving this balance is the formula for Economic Order Quantities (EOQ), which is :

$$EOQ = \sqrt{\frac{2RS}{KC}}$$

Where,

R = Annual stock used in units

S = Order preparation cost in Rupees.

K = Cost of carrying inventory as percentage of inventory.

C = Cost per unit.

As to the size of a production run, the small manufacturer can easily apply the following formula for Economic Production Quantities (EPQ), which is :

$$EPQ = \sqrt{\frac{2RC}{K(1-\frac{r}{p})}}$$

Where,

R = Annual units required.

C = Cost of setup (of machinery)

K = Cost of holding inventory (stock)

r = Rate that units are used in time period.

p = Rate units are produced in same time period.

(b) Small Retail Trader

The typical retailer is an artist in trading and stocking huge quantities and varieties of merchandise. This requires accurate records and frequent observations to control the situation.

There are two kinds of inventory records is Perpetual Inventory Control and Physical count. First Perpetual system as used in Inventory Control means that the balance on hand is shown after every stock record entry. In the following (illustration) of a stock book for Retailer in a tabular form, which includes all such things a dealer needs is a columnar book showing the following information.

Stock Book in Perpetual Inventory Control System

Date	In	Out	Balance
Jan. 1. 2004	-	-	500 Nos.
Jan. 6. 2004	-	80	420 Nos.
Jan. 8. 2004	-	40	380 Nos.
Jan. 9. 2004	-	50	330 Nos.
Jan. 10. 2004	-	60	270 Nos.
Jan. 11. 2004	-	40	230 Nos.
Jan. 14. 2004	1000 Nos.	20	1210 Nos.
Jan. 15. 2004	-	30	1180 Nos.
Jan. 16. 2004	-	100	1080 Nos.
Jan. 18. 2004	-	60	1020 Nos.
Jan. 19. 2004	-	40	980 Nos.
Jan. 20. 2004	-	70	910 Nos.
Etc. to Jan. 31st 2004	-	500	410 Nos.
Total	1000	1090	

In the above illustration a. retailer may have the 'Ins' which records are obtained from the manufacturers invoices/whole sellers invoices and the 'outs' are inserted from a daily total of the sales invoices.

The second type of inventory (stock) control records are those that show the following information about an item in stock through physical count :

1. Description, model number, size/colour etc.
2. Number on hand.
3. Number ordered and received.
4. Number available.
5. Number sold.
6. Number on hand (Balance on hand at the last date).

Inventory Control Record Card

Date	6/1/04	14/1/04	18/1/04	18/1/04		1/2/04
Model	On hand	Ordered	Received	Available	Sold	Stock in hand
BW-4	2	2	2	4	1	3
BW-5	6	0	0	6	5	1
BW-6	3	3	2	5	3	2
Totals	11	5	4	15	9	6

The above illustrated method is not so much a way of controlling inventory as it is a method of adjusting the inventory figure on the books to the physical inventory control at the end of an accounting period. It is simple and saves book-keeping expenses.

(c) Wholesaler

The problem of wholesaler's in inventory control are different from those of the retailer. As wholesalers generally carry much larger inventories and fill order to the manufacturer/producers directly of a greater magnitude. Wholesalers must keep extremely accurate records. Wholesalers do not have to display of merchandise, they do face serious storage problems as yesterday's large empty spaces become overcrowded with today's merchandise.

The typical wholesaler inventory control system provides the same information as the retail system. This, merchandise on hand, on order, order received, sold and stock on hand etc. Other than this detailed record of inventory a wholesalers have to maintain a minimum stock requirement that triggers future buying. Wholesalers may use a tickler file (Hurman, 1979) to remind them when to order and a stock record and renewal form as shown in the following illustration.

Stock Record and Renewal Form

Source ....Item :..................................

	RECEIVED		SOLD		Balance
Date	Order No.	Units	Invoice No.	Units	On hand
10/9	0.146	200			216
16/9	-	-	S. 164	48	168
17/9	0.149	80	-	-	248
22/9	0.151	80	-	-	328
24/9	-	-	S. 181	200	128
Minimum stock level		200 Units	Recorder Level		40 Units

It is very important for all retailers, as wholesalers who run small businesses must carry a supply and the proper assortment of all items to meet any anticipated demands. Otherwise they may loses sales which will ultimately suffer profits. On the other hand, if the business organisation does not have a balanced stock of all the items he sells regularly, a merchant might very well have too much capital tied up in slow moving items. This will seriously affect the business's 'stock-turnover'.

There is no possible way for a stock/inventory of any reasonable size to keep control of these important functions, other than by adequate stock records, especially if the maximum and minimum stock requirements are based on several years actual experience (Tungale, 1952). A careful scrutiny of each stock card will give useful information regarding the high and low movement of each item; how many units are being sold each month, 'the efficiency with which merchandise is being purchased; and finally, the most valuable information the stock card will give – the items which have been in stock too long.

If all the information caught in time, an over-stock position can be adjusted at a minimum of loss. It is obvious that the later the discovery of such a situation, the greater the potential loss.

CHAPTER SIX

FINANCIAL MANAGEMENT PRACTICES OF SMALL BUSINESS: DATA ANALYSIS AND INTERPRETATION

With a view to achieve the objectives of the present study, the 191 duly filled in correct questionnaire are processed for the purpose of analysis and interpretation in this chapter. The detailed breakup of the sample data state-wise were already shown in Chapter–I under the head Research Methodology. In Chapter–V, the various tools and techniques of financial management has been explained and the present chapter examines the practices of small business of these tools and techniques in North-Eastern region. Initially, the basic characteristic of the sample unit were examined followed by examination of awareness level and uses of these financial tools and techniques in decision making and their impact on achievement level of those small businesses. Moreover, the practices and the performance (perceived) of small business units in relation to their characteristic are also examined and tested statistically.

Sample Characteristics

In order to provide an insight into how small business units operate and to compare financial management practices of different types of businesses, the small businesses in the sample (N=191) have been analysed in terms of :

i) Age of Owner-Manager

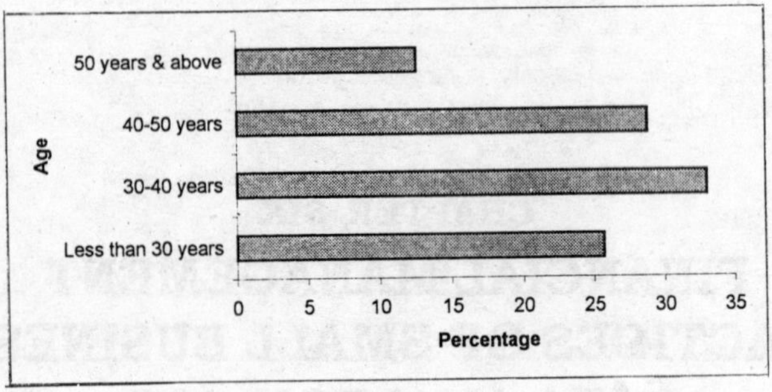

Fig. 1

ii) Sex of the Owner-Manager

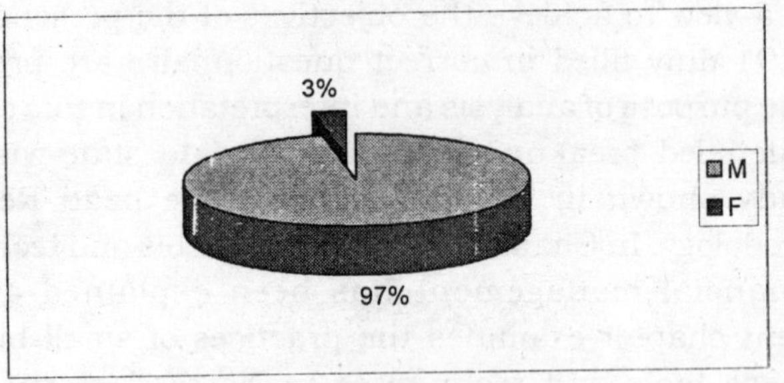

Fig. 2

iii) Location of Small Business

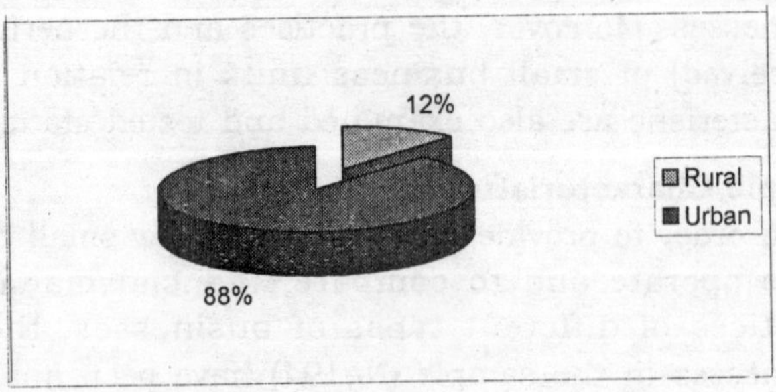

Fig. 3

iv) Size of the Small Business Units according to Number of Employees

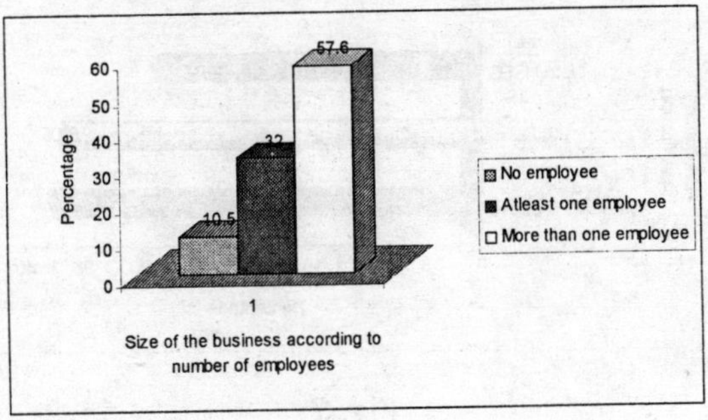

Fig. 4

v) Age of the Business Units

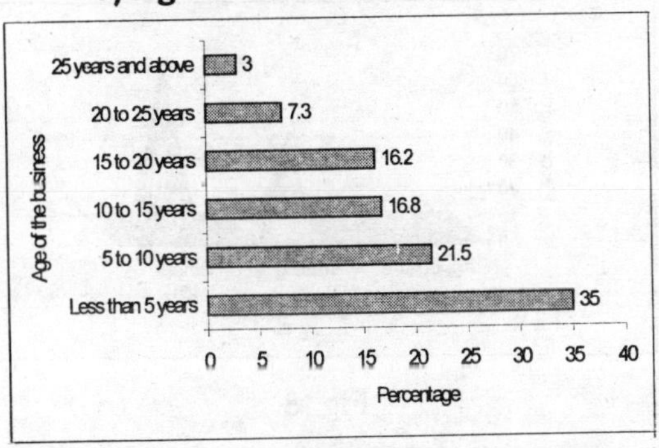

Fig. 5

vi) Small Business Units Registration position

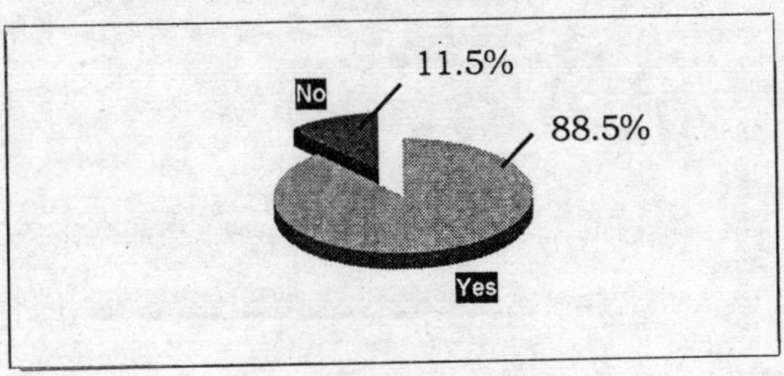

Fig. 6

vii) Educational Qualification of Owner-Managers

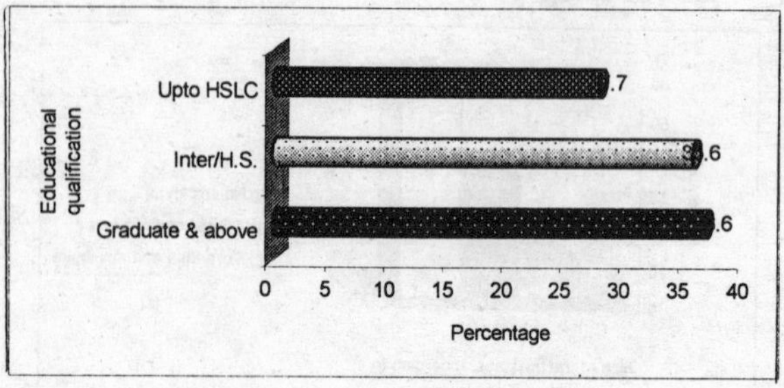

Fig. 7

viii) Owner-Managers Family Background

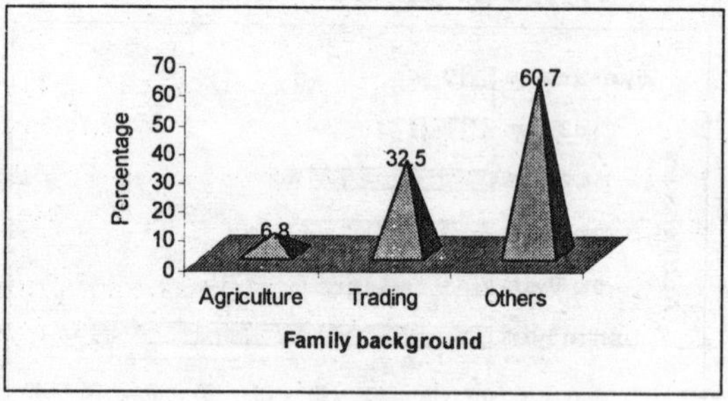

Fig. 8

ix) Owner-Managers Business Experience

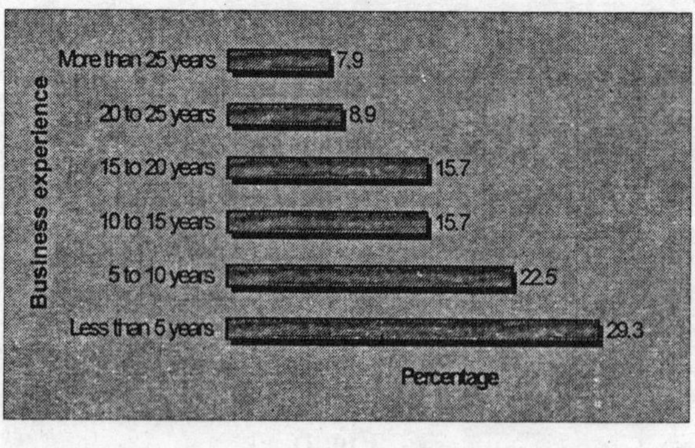

Fig. 9

x) Type of Ownership

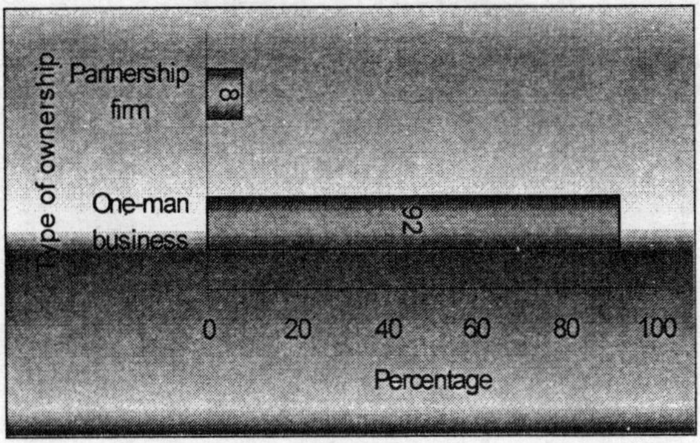

Fig. 10

xi) Principal Activity of the Business

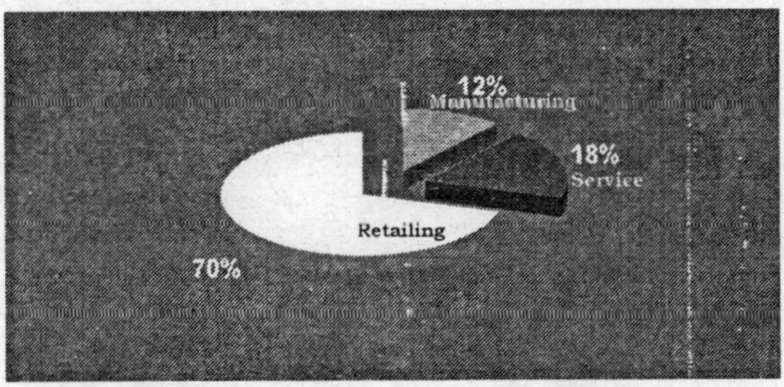

Fig. 11

xii) Principal Market for the Small Business products

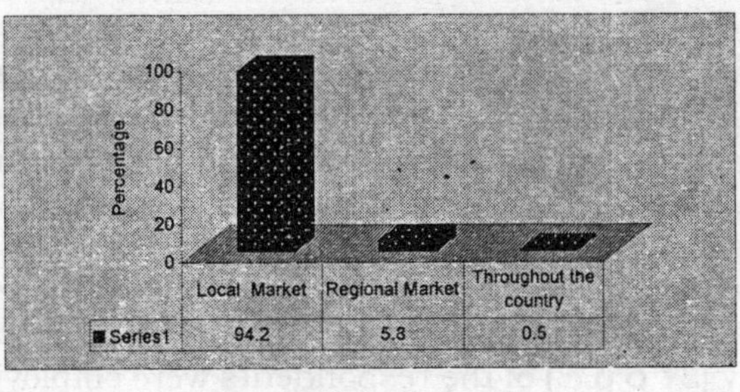

Fig.12

xiii) Owner-Managers Perception about their Business Performance/Achievement

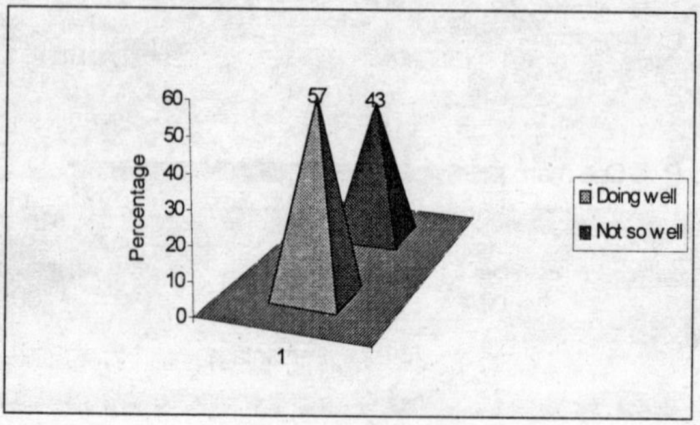

Fig.13

xiv) Monthly sales turnover of the Small Business Units

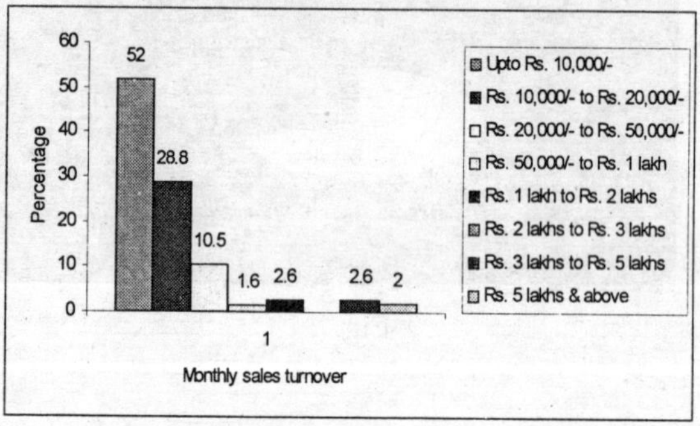

Fig.14

Demographically, 97 p.c. of the owner-managers of small business under study were male and only 3 p.c. were female. More than half of the businesses were over 5 years of age (65 p.c.). Majority (92 p.c.) of the businesses were one man business i.e. sole proprietorship business; only 8 p.c. of the units were found partnership firms (more than one owner); and no company form of business were there in the study. Majority (57.6 p.c.) of the respondents were employing more than one employees. Nearly 60.7 p.c. of the respondents had a family background other than business, while 32.5 p.c. operated family-oriented enterprises.

The majority of the owner managers had educational credentials not relevant to their enterprises' activity, as all of the owner-managers under study had general educational qualification, like graduation (36.6 p.c.), Inter/HS (36.6 p.c.) and upto HSLC (27.7 p.c.); no technically qualified professionals were found in the survey.

The small business units of North-Eastern Region of India including Assam mostly (92 p.c.) operate in the local market i.e. to meet the local market demand. Nearly 88 p.c. of the respondents were registered units (Registered under local authority i.e. Municipal Corporation, Municipal Board, Sales Tax etc.)

As it was observed from the study, that principal activity of the small businesses were trading (70.2 p.c.) in North-Eastern region of India.

In relation to size, more than half (52 p.c.) of the business enterprises reported monthly sales revenue of upto Rs. 10,000/-; only 4 (2 p.c.) enterprises where monthly revenue earning was more than Rs. 5 lakhs.

Analysis according to the features of the Business :

Table 6.1

Age of the Small Business and their perceived level of Achievement

Age of the Business	Doing well (N – 109)	Not Doing well (N – 82)
Less than 5 years of Age	38%	32%
More than 5 years of Age	62%	68%

To find out the relationship between age of the business and their achievement, the null-hypothesis was taken, that is, the two attributes age of the business and the level of performance or achievement is not associated or independent of each others influence (Table 6.1).

The result of χ^2 (Chi-square) test revealed that, Table value of χ^2 for 1df (degree of freedom) at 5 % level of significance is 3.148 and calculated value is 0.71707.

Since calculated value of χ^2 (Chi-square) is less than tabulated value, so we can accept our hypothesis, that the age of the business and the performance or achievement of the business unit were independent or insignificant.

Table 6.2
Business Sector and their perceived level of Achievement

Business Sector	Doing well (N – 109)	Not Doing well (N – 82)
Manufacturing	8%	16%
Service Sector	22%	13%
Retail Trading	70%	71%

In order to find out the relationship between business sector and their perceived level of performances/ achievement, our null-hypothesis was that the two attributes i.e. business sector (Manufacturing/Service/ Retail Trading) and their level of performance is independent or not associated (Table 6.2).

The χ^2 (Chi-square) test revealed that, Table value of χ^2 for 2df at 5% level of significance is 5.992 and calculated value of χ^2 is 18.115.

It seems that the calculated value of χ^2 is much higher than this table value and hence the result does not support the hypothesis or reject the hypothesis.

We can thus conclude that different business sector has some relationship with their performance. As the tabulated data (Table 6.2) revealed that nearly 68.5 p.c. of the service sector were doing well while nearly 59 p.c. of the sample units under manufacturing sector were not performing well according the perceived level of achievement. On the other hand 57 p.c. of the retail traders were performing well.

Table 6.3

Age of the Business and the size (according to their monthly turnover)

Size of the Business (According to monthly turnover)	Less than 5 years old (N – 67)	More than 5 years old (N – 124)
(1) Upto Rs. 10,000/-	75%	39.5%
(2) Rs. 10,000/- to Rs. 20,000/-	16%	35.5%
(3) Rs. 20,000/- to Rs. 50,000/-	6%	13%
(4) Rs. 50,000/- and above	3%	12%

To see if there was any correlation between two attributes i.e. size of the business and their age, the null-hypothesis is that these two attributes are independent (Table 6.3).

The table value of χ^2 for 3df (degree of freedom) at 5% level of significance is 7.813 and the calculated value of χ^2 is 21.89.

Therefore, it shows that, the calculated value of χ^2 is much higher than this table value which means that the calculated value cannot be said to have arisen just because of chance. It is significant. Hence, the hypothesis does not hold good or is rejected.

This means that, there is some relationship between size and the age of the business units. From the data (Table 6.3) it is revealed that the size in terms of (monthly) sales volume increases with relation to their ages. From Table 6.3 it appears that younger business (less than 5 years old) are generally small in size in terms of turnover, i.e. 75 p.c. of the younger business are having a monthly turnover of Rs. 10,000 only. On the other hand, older business (more than 5 years old) are found to be bigger in size in terms of turnover, around 60 p.c. of the older business having a turnover of more than Rs. 10,000 per month. The corresponding figure for the younger business is 25 p.c. Therefore, we can come to the conclusion that as the age of the business increases their sales turnover may also increase relatively to some extent.

Table 6.4
Business Experience by the owner-manager and perceived level of achievement/performance

Business Experience	Doing well (N – 109)	Not doing well (N – 82)
Less than 5 years	31%	27%
5 years to 10 years	20%	26%
10 years to 15 years	15.6%	16%
15 years to 20 years	18%	12%
20 years to 25 years	5.5%	13%
25 years and above	9%	6%

To know if there was any co-relation between two attributes i.e. business experience and achievement of the business (Doing well/Not doing well) - χ^2 (Chi-square) test was undertaken (Table 6.4).

Calculated value of χ^2 is 5.89975 while table value for 5df (degree of freedom) at 5% level of significance is 11.07.

It seems that the calculated value of χ^2 (Chi-square) is less than tabulated value. So, we can come to the conclusion that business experience of owner-manager of small business has no relationship with the business performances/achievement. This two attributes are independent.

6.2. Results of the study

The responses collected during interview have been analysed to focus on the information available to the small businesses in relation to :

1. Awareness level of owner-managers.

2. Basic accounting record for day to day monitoring of business performance.
3. Creditors and Debtors Records.
4. Working capital management.
5. Costing records.
6. Inventory management.
7. Auditing.
8. Tax matters.
9. Capital expenditure decision.
10. Sources of finance.
11. Drawing decisions.

The following financial management tools and techniques although very important and relevant in financial management of small business but suprisingly not a single unit was found to be practicing the tools. Therefore the researcher could not analysis data and information relating to this tools and techniques in the present study.

- Budgeting
- CVP Analysis
- Ratio Analysis
- Fund Flow Statement
- Costing System / Methods
- Inventory Control Techniques / Methods
- Investment Management
- Techniques of Capital Budgeting

It is pertinent to mention here that although their awareness level is poor and do not use above techniques, but to access the decision making process of owner-manager the researcher included some related question to a certain the decision making behaviour of owner-manager of small business in north-eastern region of India.

Again each of the above 11 (eleven) aspects were examined in terms of :

(a) Theoretical considerations.

(b) General survey findings about the practice of firms in the survey.

(c) The difference between the small business firms on the basis of age, size, business sector etc.

1. Awareness level of owner-managers

The present study has identified 27 (twenty seven) most commonly used financial management tools and techniques and tried to judge the level of awareness of the owner-manager.

The result of the study shows that only 12 (twelve) tools/ techniques of financial management were known by the small businesses owner-managers of North-Eastern Region of India out of 27 (twenty seven) techniques identified for the study. Again out of these 12 (twelve) known instrument of financial management barring Cash Book, Debtors Book and Creditors Book (100 p.c. awareness); awareness level on other tools and techniques of financial management were very low.

To run a business successfully, it is necessary to keep accurate, correct and systematic financial records in time. The main objective of financial data is to provide information to the owner-manager to make wise and informed decision. But the findings of the study revealed that the awareness level on financial management techniques, of small businesses owner managers was very poor. So, we can say that financial data recording system, which is the key functional area of a business, was almost a neglected area of business management in North Eastern Region of India including Assam.

It was surprising to note that only 34 p.c. of the respondent were aware about financial statements (profit and loss account/balance sheet). It was possible to run a business because of small size. This low level of awareness and thereby preparation of financial statements may be an important cause of low level of performance and growth of small businesses of the region in the long run.

Considering other financial management tools for future decision making it was observed that, no respondents were aware and also used the budgetary control- techniques, to manage their firms, and used for future planning and control. This result were consistent with Mirze (1979) who found that the degree of awareness and use of budgeting was low in Northern Australia and the firm size affected its use. Small businesses were reluctant to utilise budgeting techniques as they were not aware of their usefulness in the business and also lack of knowledge and understanding of their utilities in business future planning and control.

It was observed that only 11.5 p.c. of the respondent were aware of the formal method of Inventory (Stock) record, through stores ledger. Owner-managers opined that they generally did their stock verified through physical stock verification process, which is self and tailor-made process. No formalised or the perpetual inventory management methods were used.

All of the respondent indicate that they were not aware of cost control methods and future planning measures for the business and therefore, there was no use of these instruments - like, Budgeting (capital / sales / purchase / cash), Job costing, process costing, Break even analysis etc.

Regarding financial planning, and control techniques like liquidity, leverage and activity measures, the level of awareness was very poor among the respondents. According to Holmes (1986) the responsibility for using financial management, tools generally rest upon owner-manager of a small business as the owner-managers of small business were unaware of the techniques therefore, proper and judged use of this instrument for analysis did not apply to the small business of this region; since these instruments of financial management requires an in-depth understanding of the preparation of financial statements.

Table – 6.I

Awareness level of owner-manager of Small Business of North-Eastern region of India.

Financial management tools in practice	Awareness level (N=191)
Purchase Ledger	20%
Sales Ledger	11%
Cash Book	100%
Debtors Book	100%
Creditors Book	100%
Depreciation	15.7%
Trial Balance	-
Bank Reconciliation Statement	5.2%
Profit and Loss Statement	34%
Balance sheet	34%
Sales / Purchase Budget	-
Capital Budgeting	-
Cost-volume-profit (CVP) Analysis	-
Job Costing System	-
Process Costing system	-
Inventory Control Method (EOQ, ABC analysis, FIFO, LIFO etc.)	-
Stores Ledger	11.5%
Liquidity measures through Ratio analysis (Financial Ratios), Liquidity Ratios,, Quick Ratio, Capital gearing ratio, debt-equity-ratio etc.	-
Fund flow analysis	-
Comparative financial statement analysis	-
Working capital management	-
Calculation of cost of capital	-
Pay back method of analysis (NPV) and Internal rate of return (IRR)	-
Auditing	5.7%
Tax matters	77%
Investment management	-

Table – 6.II
Educational qualification of owner-manager and level of awareness

Financial management tools in practice	Graduate and above (N=70)	HS/ Inter (N=68)	Upto HSLC (N=53)
Purchase Ledger	29%	22%	5%
Sales Ledger	17.1%	12%	3%
Cash Book	100%	100%	100%
Debtors Book	100%	100%	100%
Creditors Book	100%	100%	100%
Depreciation	26%	26%	11%
Trial Balance	-	-	-
Bank Reconciliation Statement	10%	2%	1%
Profit and Loss Statement	50%	25%	23%
Balance sheet	50%	25%	23%
Sales / Purchase Budget	-	-	-
Capital Budgeting	-	-	-
Cost-volume-profit (CVP) Analysis	-	-	-
Job Costing System	-	-	-
Process Costing system	-	-	-
Inventory Control Method (EOQ, ABC analysis, FIFO, LIFO etc.)	-		-
Stores Ledger	19%	12%	1%
Liquidity measures through Ratio analysis (Financial Ratios), Liquidity Ratios,, Quick Ratio, Capital gearing ratio, debt-equity-ratio etc.	-	-	-
Fund flow analysis	-	-	-
Comparative financial statement analysis	-	-	-
Working capital management	-	-	-
Calculation of cost of capital	-	-	-
Pay back method of analysis (NPV) and Internal rate of return (IRR)	-	-	-
Auditing	7%	6%	4%
Tax matters	83%	74%	75%
Investment management	-	-	-

Table – 6.III
Business Experience (Age) and the level of awareness of the owner-managers

Financial Management tools in practices	Less than 5 years	5 to 15 years	15 to 25 years	25 years and above
Purchase Ledger	3.5%	25%	28%	33%
Sales Ledger	3.5%	8%	17%	33%
Cash Book	100%	100%	100%	100%
Debtors Book	100%	100%	100%	100%
Creditors Book	100%	100%	100%	100%
Depreciation	Nil	14%	42.5%	80%
Trial Balance				
Bank Reconciliation Statement		2.7%	8.5%	27%
Profit and Loss Statement	3.5%	27%	60%	93%
Balance Sheet	3.5%	27%	60%	93%
Sales/Purchase Budget	-	-	-	-
Capital Budgeting	-	-	-	-
Cost Volume Profit (CVP) Analysis	-	-	-	-
Job Costing System	-	-	-	-
Process Costing System	-	-	-	-
Inventory Control Method (EOQ, ABC analysis, FIFO, LIFO etc.)				
Stores Ledger		14%	21%	13%
Liquidity measures through Ratio analysis (Financial Ratios), Liquidity Ratios, Quick Ratio, Capital gearing Ratio, Debt-Equity-Ratio etc.				
Fund flow analysis				
Comparative financial statement analysis				
Working capital management				
Calculation of cost of capital				
Pay back method of project analysis (ROI)				
Net present value method of analysis (NPV) and Internal Rate of Return (IRR)				
Auditing		2.7%	13%	20%
Tax matters	57%	79%	91%	100%
Investment Management				

In North Eastern Region of India, lack of understanding of the benefits of using Ratio analysis, the ability to interpret financial statements and capital investment appraisal techniques thereby apply them to management decision making was highly constrained. This result tends to confirm the findings of Grablowsky and William (1980) that small businesses owner-managers, do not use these techniques of business financial appraisal because they find these highly quantitative.

A cursory look into the following table reflect a very important phenomena in relation to level of awareness and educational qualification of the owner-manager, although level of awareness about the financial management tools and techniques in general is very low but the study observed that higher the educational qualification better is the awareness level.

Another interesting phenomena about the level of awareness observed is that experienced owner-manager are more aware about the financial management tools and techniques than the less or younger business owner-manager.

2. Basic Accounting Records for day to day monitoring of business :

Running a business effectively requires awareness and knowledge by the owner-manager of a small business on a day to day basis about how the business is doing. Apart from legal requirement (by the tax authorities, bankers, investors and others), there is a practical necessity to keep sufficient records to ensure that business activity can continue without problem. If an owner-manager of a small business has no knowledge of which bills are outstanding for payment and of the extent of credit; and also keeps no record for how much is due to the business from customers, what is the present position of the business, then he will not stay long in the business. If the business unit regularly runs into cash problem (short of cash) because the organisation has no proper control or accurate record of bank and cash balances, this will alienate the banker and the creditor or both. Therefore, these historical informations, which are generated in the day-to-day business activities; are the vital economic data/information helping to take proper and adequate future decisions.

It follows from this that all firms should be expected to keep a record of daily cash receipts and payments because such records are important for a business. This daily receipts and payments, usually recorded in a 'Cash Book'; and information about those to whom business firm owes money (Creditors) and those who owe money to the business (Debtors) should be recorded separately. In order to be able to use Accounting records to provide information, these business information in the form of financial data, need to be written up frequently. However, the fields of accounting and finance have yet to provide an accepted normative theory indicating which financial reports are most valuable in financial management and how often they should be used (McMahon and Davies, 1994).

Survey Results

The question in the survey which related to Basic Record keeping were :

Question (Q) : How do you measure Financial Performance of your Business?

Response (R) : The study observed that 51.3 p.c. of the small business units under study, measure their performances on the basis of 'Sales' i.e. total amount of sales during a particular period of time. Only 43 p.c. of the respondent use profit and sales (both) to evaluate their business performances.

Q : What is the frequency of preparing financial Accounting records ?

R : The survey result revealed that, only 15 p.c. of the small business units of North-Eastern region of India kept their Accounting information upto date on a daily basis; 36 p.c. on a monthly basis and 49 p.c. i.e. majority of them update their accounting records on annual basis.

Table 6.5
Tools of measurement of Financial Performance of by the Small Business Units

Tools	Used
Sales	51.3%
Expenses	-
ROI	-
Budget vs. Actual profit	-
Profit	
Profit and Sales	43%

Table 6.6
Frequency of Preparing Financial records

Frequency of record keeping	p.c. of owner-manager
Daily	15
Weekly	-
Monthly	36
Yearly	49
Never	-

Table 6.7
Perceived level of performance and frequency of record keeping by the Small Business

Frequency of preparing / Financial Records	Level of Achievement	
	Doing well (N – 109)	No doing well (N – 82)
Daily	17%	12%
Weekly	NIL	NIL
Monthly	29%	44%
Yearly	53%	43%

N.B. : One unit of above 8 years of age did not prepare accounts. Not a single unit was found that prepared its accounts weekly.

To know if there was any relationship between two attributes i.e. frequency of record keeping and level of achievement, χ^2 (Chi-square) test was used. The null-hypothesis of the study is that these two attributes are independent (Table 6.7)

The calculated value of χ^2 is 4.6921 and Table Value of χ^2 for 2df (degree of freedom) at 5% (p.c.) level of significance is 5.992.

From the result, it is observed that, calculated value of χ^2 (Chi-square) is less than tabulated value. Therefore, we accept our hypothesis and draw the conclusion that, the level of achievement (perceived)/ level of performance and frequency of record keeping has no relationship i.e. they were independent.

But, firms doing well were more likely to be comfortable with accounts and much more likely to keep their books upto date at least and yearly (53 p.c.) basis.

Table 6.8
Age of the Small Business and frequency of record keeping

Frequency	Age of the Business	
	Less than 5 (five) years old (N – 67)	More than 5(five) years old (N – 124
Daily	4.5%	21%
Weekly	-	-
Monthly	28%	36%
Yearly	67%	42%

Present study has taken the null-hypothesis that the two attributes i.e. age of the business unit and frequency of record keeping is independent (Table – 6.8).

The result of χ^2 (Chi-square) test – Table Value of χ^2 for

2df (degree of freedom) at 5% level of significance is 5.992 and calculated value is 14.02.

From the result, it is observed that, calculated value of χ^2 is higher than the table value and the result does not support the hypothesis.

Therefore, we can say that age of the business and frequency of record keeping has some relationship. As the (Table 6.8) data revealed that nearly 21 p.c. of more than 5 years old small business units wrote up their books of account daily compared to younger (less than 5 years old) business (4.5 p.c.). Similarly nearly 36 p.c. of older business (more than 5 years of age) maintain their books monthly compared to younger business (28 p.c.) which would seemed often enough for most types of the firms to monitor their affairs.

Q : Who writes up your Accounting records ?

When designing the research, it was thought that those who wrote up their books themselves might be more in touch with the business. However, it was discovered that owner-managers who know most about their business did not necessarily write up their own books of accounts. According to the study 63.35 p.c. of the respondents keep their books of accounts themselves, Manager (employee) keeps 9.4 p.c., Accountants 8.4 p.c. and Part-time Accountant 18.8 p.c. (Table 6.9)

Table 6.9

Writing of Books of Accounts

Myself	63.35%
Manager	9.4%
Accountant (Permanent employee)	8.4%
Part-time Accountant	18.8%

Q : Is a computer used to keep business records ?

R : In case of use of computer, it was observed that only 11 p.c. of the respondents uses computer in maintaining their daily accounting records. It was also found that 8.5 p.c. of the business units under service sector and 4.5 p.c. in the manufacturing units and 12 p.c. of the Trading units were using computers for record keeping. It might be expected that firms with more complex business and larger small businesses among the small business units, would be more likely to have a computer.

Table 6.10

Use of Computer by the Small Business Units in their Accounts keeping

Used	11%
Not used	89%

Business sector	Computer used in p.c.
Manufacturing	4.5
Service	8.5
Trading	12

Q : What are the different books that are maintained by the business units ?

R : As expected, the majority (100 p.c.) of the small businesses kept a Cash Book since a Cash Book is necessary for any business to keep a track of the cash balance and also know the amounts which are being received and paid.

Table 6.11

Common financial accounting tools used by small business

Name of Accounting books	Used
Sales Book	9.4%
Purchases Book	12.5%
Cash Book	100%
Debtors Book	100%
Creditors Book	100%
Ledger	-
Profit and Loss A/c	24.6%
Balance sheet	10.5%

Although, whatever records were kept were generally based on the traditional "Mahajani System" which is incomplete in nature (mostly under single entry system, and conversion into double entry is very difficult as records are kept haphazardly). It was also observed in the study, in most of the cases, except those using computerised accounting system (i.e. only 11 p.c.); rough works like 'tokas' (slips) etc. as accounting records. The 'tokas' usually hand written. Most of the accounting records were written in one general ledger or Register, incorporating various kinds of business accounting information, whether it be cash, credit or other forms of transaction.

While looking into the most common accounting instrument in use by the small business units (Table – 6.11), the study found that only 24.6 p.c. of the respondents prepared Profit and Loss Account for the business. There was a question in the survey about the owner-manager's behaviour of assigning their business performance, it was found that nearly 43% of the respondents assess their business performance on the basis of profit. But, it was observed 24.6 p.c. of the small business units prepare Profit and Loss Account, and therefore, nearly 75 p.c. of the respondents assess their business performance on observation. It was also discovered during the study that small businesses whose turnover is more than Rs. 1 lakh, all of them (100 p.c.) prepare Profit and Loss Account for their business. This observation signifies that majority of the smaller units are most likely, not preparing the Profit and loss Accounts. This ultimately may give wrong signal to the business owner-managers as they do not know the present position of the business. This implies that Profit and Loss Account has little/no utility/relevance for the owner-manager to take stock as an information base to take future decisions.

In regard to preparation of Balance Sheet, only 10.5 p.c. of the surveyed units prepare Balance Sheet for their firm, of which 64.3 p.c. were the small business units whose turnover were more than Rs. 1 lakh. Therefore, it can be concluded that small units whose sales turnover is less were more reluctant to prepare Profit and Loss Account and Balance Sheet.

Table 6.12

Level of Education (of the owner-manager) and use of financial management tools and techniques.

Tools and Techniques of financial management	Graduate and above (N – 70)	Inter/ HS pass 12th standard (N – 68)	Upto 10th standard (N – 53)
Profit and loss account	41%	15%	15%
Balance sheet	20%	4.4%	7.5%
Stores Ledger	17%	6%	5.7%

N.B. : Cash Book, Debtors Book and Creditors Book were kept by all (100 p.c.) of the sample units.

To know if there was any co-relation between two attributes i.e. level of education of owner-manager and use of financial management tools and techniques - χ^2 (Chi-square) test was undertaken to see that, this two attributes were independent or not (Table – 6.12).

Calculated value of χ^2 is 0.51238 while Table Value of χ^2 for 4df (degree of freedom) at 5 p.c. level of significance is 9.43.

It seems that the calculated value of χ^2 (Chi-square) is less than tabulated value. Therefore, we can accept our hypothesis that the level of education of owner-managers of small businesses and use of financial management tools and techniques were independent or has no significant difference with regard to use of financial tools and techniques between educated and less educated owner-managers of small businesses.

Q : What system of accounting is followed in recording of financial data ?

R : The financial data of small business under survey were mostly (90.5 p.c.) kept in single entry system or indigenous (Mahajanis) system, which is tailor made – based on the requirement and the nature of the business. This system is easy to prepare and understand. Double entry system of book-keeping were followed only in those units where computerised data entry system were prevailing (only 10.05 p.c. of small businesses).

3. Creditors and Debtors records

Responses to the questions on creditors and debtors balances show that more respondents had information about their creditors and debtors than had formal records of them. As according to the survey 100 p.c. of the respondents keep a record of creditors as well as debtors. It was also observed that 98.4 p.c. of the respondents follow the traditional method of selling which includes cash as well as credit sales. Liberal credit policy is one of the many factors that influences the demand for firms product and hence increased sales.

Question was asked on the method of credit sales. It was observed that all the respondents (98.4 p.c.) who allowing credit to their customers generally follow open account i.e. without following any credit policy. They did not study the credit worthiness of a customer. No structured credit policy were framed to study the credit worthiness on the issue of sales of goods on credit. Past business experiences was considered to be the only risk assessment technique used to evaluate the credit worthiness of a customer/person.

Not a single unit under study made provision for Bad and Doubtful debts for irrecoverable amount from debtors.

Methods of Selling

Methods	Uses in p.c.
Cash only	1.6
Credit sales only	-
Cash and Credit sales	98.4

4. Working Capital Management

Question was asked whether the respondent could separate their private assets and expenses from their business assets as well as expenses. It was surprising to discover that not a single unit could make difference between those two. They argued that, if it was their own business, then separation between business and personal expenses, is of no use.

Cash flow statements were not prepared by any of the respondents.

While discussing the financial health of the business, it was found that reserve funds were not created by any small businesses under study. As according to practice and accounting norms reserves or retained earnings is the source of finance in the years of difficulty or to extend the business in future.

Nearly all respondents (100 p.c.) said that they did not use any technique/tool of financial management like ratio analysis, CVP analysis etc. to analyse their business performances.

Analysis by features of the business about basic record keeping

Table 6.13

Basic Record keeping : Analysis by the features of the businesses.

	Age of the business		Business Sector			Achievement	
Basic Accounting Records for proper financial management	Less than 5(five) years (N – 67)	More than 5(five) years (N – 124)	Manufa-ctuing (N – 22)	Retail Trade (N – 134)	Service (N – 35)	Doing well (N – 109)	Not doing well (N–82)
Self kept	90%	49%	45.5%	68%	57%	60.5%	67%
Computer used	3%	14.5%	4.5%	11.9%	8.5%	15.6%	3.7%
Profit and loss a/c	6%	35%	45%	24%	14%	28%	19.5%
Balance sheet	3%	14.5%	13.6%	11%	5.7%	15.6%	3.6%

Note : The percentages are not additive.

Age of the business

There was significance different with regard to basic record keeping techniques between firms which were less than 5 years old and those more than 5 years old. Nearly 90 p.c. of the young (less than 5 years old) firms kept their accounts by themselves. While 49 p.c. older business firms (more than 5 years age) kept business accounts themselves (Table.– 6.13).

Interestingly although only 11 p.c. of the total sample units used computer in accounts record keeping, 14.5 p.c. of older businesses (more than 5 years old) used computer while only 3 p.c. of younger units has computer for financial data recording. Perhaps this indicate that people just starting up in small businesses are not likely to think of using a computer from the start, whereas already established businesses barring a few years of business experience would have to change their routines to begin to use a computer.

One of the basic financial statement of a business appraisal is Profit and Loss Account and Balance Sheet. While analysing on the basis of age of the business it was observed that only 6 p.c. of the younger business units (less than 5 years old) prepare Profit and Loss account and 3 p.c. of them prepare Balance Sheet. In contrast 35 p.c. of the older (more than 5 years old) business prepare profit and loss account and 14.5 p.c. prepare balance sheet. The study indicates that older business units were more knowledgeable about their business performances and record keeping than younger business.

Business Sector

The analysis shows interesting features about the different types of business. The retailer, who have the least complex decision processes, seemed the most diligent record keeper. Nearly, 68 p.c. of them kept their accounts themselves, and they all (100 p.c.) kept a cash book, debtors book and creditors book. Regarding use of computer in record keeping, nearly 12 p.c. of them (retailer) had computers, which is highest among all other sectors (manufacturer and service).

Manufacturing firms tend to have the longest lead time between paying for raw materials and effective sales. So it would be expected of them to keep more records. But the study revealed that 46 p.c. of the manufacturers kept their records by themselves – only one firm used computer for data recording. While compared to other two sectors in preparation of basic accounting statements i.e. Service and Retail sector, manufacturing units were preparing Profit and Loss Account, nearly 14 p.c. of them also used balance sheet to monitor their business performance.

Service firms were most likely to keep their accounts by themselves (57 p.c.). Although all the service firms know their creditors and debtor payment period and amount as they all (100 p.c.) kept the accounting records of these two items. Insignificant percent of this sector prepare Profit and Loss and Balance Sheet.

Level of Achievement

There was no such difference between firms doing well and not doing well in keeping the books of accounts by the owner-manager. But in the use of computer, nearly 16 p.c. of the firms doing well were using computer compared to only 4 p.c. in case of firms not doing well. This indicate that level of performance (perceived) or achievement were one of the motivating factor for small businesses to take up a computer for the business. In case of preparing profit and loss and balance sheet for the business, the study observed that firms doing well were more in number than firms not doing well. The most revealing insight from this analysis is that those not doing well were not diligent enough in preparing financial statements, like Profit and Loss and Balance Sheet, which are the most important financial tool for business performance appraisal and future decision making and planning.

Table 6.14
Size of the business (according to monthly turnover) and financial management practices.

Financial Management Tools/ Techniques	Upto Rs. 10,000/- (N – 99)	Rs. 10,000/- to Rs. 20,000/- (N – 55)	Rs. 20,000/- to Rs. 50,000/- (N – 20)	Rs. 50,000/- to Rs. 1 lakh (N – 3)	Rs. 1 lakh and above (N – 14)
Sales Book	-	1.8%	20%	100%	71%
Purchases Book	-	5.4%	35%	100%	79%
Profit and loss A/c	5%	27%	50%	100%	100%
Balance Sheet	1%	9%	20%	67%	64%
Accounts were audited (yearly)	-	-	10%	33%	57%

N.B. : Cash Book, Debtor and Creditors Books were kept by all (100 p.c.) of the small business units of North-East Region of India.

While studying the financial management practices by the small business in North-Eastern region of India, we tried to see the relationship between size of the business unit according to their monthly sales turnover and financial management tools in use.

The study revealed that (Table – 6.14), as the sales turnover increases the use of more financial tools were observed. Those small businesses were more diligent in maintaining details financial records which had more than Rs. 50,000 of monthly sales turnover. Nearly 57 p.c. of the small firms whose sales turnover more than Rs. 1 lakh, generally employed a professionally qualified auditor to audit their accounts.

5. Costing Records

If we look into the awareness level of owner-manager of small business of North-Eastern Region of India about the different financial management tools specifically for cost-control and future pricing decision, the study reveal that none of the respondents were aware of the cost-control methods like cost-volume profit analysis, job costing, process costing etc.

The questions in the survey which focus on the aforesaid aspects were:

Q. Do you make any difference between direct and indirect cost ?

Q. Can you separate your production cost into fixed and variable costs ?

Q. How are the products priced ?

Question on differentiation between direct and indirect cost was intended to see whether the owner-managers of small business units attached any importance on costing decisions. But the survey results shows that barring 3 (three) units i.e. nearly 98.4 p.c. of the respondents did not have any idea of separation between the two costs. It was also surprising discovery that except one manufacturing unit, all other units were unable to separate direct and indirect costs. As we know, separation of costs are the most important factor in pricing decision of a product and services.

Answering the question on fixed and variable costs, the survey findings shows that not a single unit could make a separation between these two costs – which is one of the most important constituent of product pricing decision.

Question on how products were priced were also considered in the study. The hourly rate was most popular with service firms and involved setting a rate per hour, which would cover the wages of the person doing the work and provide enough to pay fixed costs and earn a profit. The purchase price + percent tends to be used by retailers, where there was no recommended retail prices. Market Price is either the price the competitors were charging or the price the owner-manager, thought would be accepted as the price, which reflect the quality.

Therefore, answering to the pricing methods adopted by

the respondents, most of the firms had a good understanding of the need to build up product cost, but also pointed out that they must take account of the market. Generally following methods were used :

Table 6.15

Pricing Methods used by Small Business

Methods of Pricing	Used
(a) Full cost + P.C. of Profit	59.7%
(b) Hourly Rate	5.7%
(c) Purchase price + P.C. of Profit	27.7%
(d) Market Price	12%

In the survey, it was found that, respondents had mentioned more than one method, this was in all cases a cost based and market based response. During personal interview, some firms described how they used the cost-based method as a bench-mark, but then used their business experiences and judgement with each individual/customer as to how much more or less they could charge.

Several respondents in the Production and Service sector, pointed out that being the cheapest was not always the ideal strategy. The responses also indicated that the satisfaction enjoyed by the entrepreneur or owner-manager depends on their being able to make the decision on price and resource allocation without being answerable to anyone else.

Analysis by the features of the business

Table 6.16

Method of Pricing of products/services employed by the small business

Methods of Pricing	Manufacturing (N – 22)	Service (N –35)	Trading (N – 134)
Full cost + P.C. of Profit	68%	48.6%	61%
Hourly Rate	18%	14%	1.5%
Purchase price + P.C. of Profit	13.6%	14%	33.6%
Market	13.6%	28.5%	7.5%

To see the relationship between method of pricing and the different business sector (Manufacturing/Service/Trading) we opted for χ^2 (Chi-square) test. Null-hypothesis for the test was these two attributes were independent (Table – 6.16).

The calculated value of χ^2 is 30.7281 and Table Value of χ^2 for 6 df (degree of freedom) at 5 p.c. level of significance is 12.591.

From the result of the χ^2 Test, where calculated value is higher than the tabulated value. Therefore, the χ^2 test does not support the hypothesis. So, there is some relationship with regard to methods of price determination by different sectors of small businesses.

The χ^2 (Chi-square) Test and the Table Value show the difference between different business sectors in making pricing decisions. Manufacturing firms are much more likely to use Full Cost + P.C. of Profit (68 p.c.) than any other method. Some manufacturer are also likely to use Purchase Price + P.C. of Profit (14 p.c.) as well as market based Price (14 p.c.).

Service firms are likely to use either Full Cost (48.6 p.c.) or Market Price (28.5 p.c.) and a few use hourly rate (14 p.c.) and Purchase Price + P.C. of Profit (14 p.c.).

Retail firms use mostly either Full Cost + P.C. of Profit (61 p.c.) or Purchase Price + P.C. of Profit (34 p.c.). Although few retail firms also use market based pricing (7.5 p.c.).

6. Inventory Management

Stock records may be kept by all types of firms to help with ordering, replenishment of stock by the retail business and particularly in manufacturing firms, to monitor the costs tied up in work-in-progress and finished goods stock.

On the whole the firms in the survey were less likely to keep detailed stock records to control/management of inventory as only 10 p.c. of the respondents prepare/maintain stock records through stock register. Majority (more than 90 p.c.) of the respondents, generally follow the physical stock verification at the end of the year.

Therefore, it can be said that, small business units under study did not follow a systematic method of stores keeping. It was also observed that no inventory management techniques were used in the proper and systematic management/control of stock by any of the respondents.

Separate record keeping for Inventory Management

Yes	10%
No	90%

7. Auditing

The question asked on this topic is :

Q : Do you get your Business Accounts Audited yearly ?

R : The study showed a very poor positive response. As it was observed that only 5.5 p.c. of the small businesses get their accounts audited by a qualified Auditor. Accounts were audited only 9 p.c. of the manufacturing units, 4.5 p.c. of the trading businesses and 8.5 p.c. of the service sector units.

It was also revealed (Table – 6.17) that large among the small businesses, whose monthly turnover was more than Rs. 5 lakhs, get their accounts audited yearly. On the other hand 80 p.c. of the firms whose monthly turnover was between Rs. 3 to 5 lakhs also audit their accounts yearly.

Therefore, from the study we can say that majority (94 p.c.) of the small businesses accounts were not audited or the process of audit were not taken up.

Table 6.17
Auditing undertaken

Turnover (Monthly)	Business Sector Manufacturing (N – 22)	Trading (N – 134)	Service (N – 35)	Total (N – 191)
Upto Rs. 10,000	-	-	-	-
Rs. 10,000 to Rs. 20,000	-	-	-	-
Rs. 20,000 to Rs. 50,000	4.5%	0.7%	-	1%
Rs. 50,000 to Rs. 1 lakh	-	0.7%		0.5%
Rs. 1 lakh to Rs. 2 lakhs	-	-	-	-
Rs. 2 lakhs to Rs. 3 lakhs	-	-	-	-
Rs. 3 lakhs to Rs. 5 lakhs	-	2.4%	2.8%	2%
Rs. 5 lakhs and above	4.5%	0.7%	5.7%	2%
Total	9%	4.5%	8.5%	5.5%

8. Tax Matters :

It was found that 37.7% of the survey population maintained their tax related aspects of their business by themselves (owner-manager). On the other hand Part-time Accountant 22.5% and Tax Consultant maintained nearly 25% of the business tax matters.

Table 6.18

Tax ascertainment

Self/owner-manager	37.7%
Employees	6.8%
Part-time Accountant	22.5%
Tax Consultant	25.7%

9. Rationale for Capital Expenditure

In the survey question asked on this topic was, if you wish to purchase new equipment or assets for your business, describe how you would decide whether it was worth while ?

Table 6.19

Basis of Capital Expenditure Decisions

Necessity	51.3%
Efficiency	39.8%
Bank finance	8.9%
Bank Balance	NIL

The responses from the survey showed a very poor understanding of the capital expenditure issue by the owner-managers of small businesses. In most of the cases the capital would have to be provided by the proprietor (owner-manager), either by introducing more capital or obtaining loan from the relatives or institutional finance (banks etc.) on the pledge on their personal property.

Capital expenditure and investment decision based on prudent financial management techniques like DCF (Discounted Cash flow) method or Payback method were almost absent in case of small business in North-Eastern Region of India.

This responses from the survey demonstrate how the owner-manager's involvement in the small business made the capital investment decision making procedure an informal one. Simple observation of the business requirement was considered an important yardstick for capital investment in the business. It was also simplified by their being one decision maker (owner-manager), one beneficiary and one financier.

From the survey (Table – 6.19) it appeared that small businesses acquired their equipment or assets over time rather than at the start of their businesses. For a large group 51.3 p.c., "Necessity" was the governing factor for acquiring new assets. While personal interaction during the survey, on capital expenditure decision, one Welding Work-Shop owner-manager said, "If we can not manage without it (equipment / machinery / assets) we will buy it, but if we only use it once or twice; then we will think about hiring it". This practical response by an experienced small business owner-manager indicate that in some cases there was no choice as to whether or not to make the investment.

Nearly 39.8 p.c. of the respondents cited 'increased efficiency' as the rationale behind such a decision. All the responses in this category indicated a reluctance to spend unless tangible benefits could be seen.

Availability of bank loan/finance option was considered by 8.9 p.c. of the respondents.

Analysis by the features of the business :

Table 6.20
Rationale of Capital Expenditure Decision taken by small business.

	Age of the business		Business Sector			Achievement	
Methods	Less than 5(five) years (N – 67)	More than 5(five) years (N – 124)	Manufa-ctuing (N – 22)	Trad-ing (N – 134)	Service (N – 35)	Doing well (N – 109)	Not doing well (N – 82)
Necessity	72%	40%	45.5%	45.5%	77%	50.5%	52.5%
Efficiency	7.5%	57%	50%	44%	17%	44%	34%
Bank finance	9%	9%	4.5%	10%	6%	5%	13.5%
Bank Balance	NIL	NIL	NIL	Nil	NIL	NIL	NIL

Age of the Business

Young businesses (less than 5 years of age) were more likely to regard necessity as the most important (72 p.c.) criteria, whereas older firms (more than 5 years of age) had obtained their required equipment and would buy more, if efficiency (57 p.c.) could be improved.

Business Sector

In case of capital investment decision, different sector of the business shows different behaviour. As 77 p.c. of the service sector regarded necessity as their most important criteria, whereas 50 p.c. of the manufacturing units opined that efficiency is the most important criteria for capital investment decision model.

Level of Achievement

There was no significant difference observed on the level of achievement (doing well/not doing well) and the capital investment decision model in case of small businesses.

10. Source of finance

The question in the survey relating to source of funds apart from personal finance revealed that Bank finance was the main source of finance, as 44.5% respondents received bank loan for their business.

Table 6.21
Source of Finance

Hire Purchase	2%
Leasing	-
Venture capital fund	-
Equity capital	-
Bank loan	44.5%

Hire purchase facilities were availed by only 2% of the sampled units.

In the present study no other form of financing by the small business of this region was found although, internal sources like retained earnings bringing new capital in the form of cash or other kinds of assets introduced by the owner-manager at the time of need and trade credits might have been obtained as other major source of finance.

11. Rationale of Drawing decisions

Drawings are cash amount or normal business sale articles taken out of the business by the owner-manager (proprietor). In small businesses, the owner-managers are likely to take money/saleable articles out of the business on some regular basis for their personal needs. The method of arriving at the decision on how much to take from the business can throw light on the way owner-manager of a small business make financial decision about their firms.

Table 6.22

Rationale of Drawing decisions

Salary	NIL
Wages+Bonus	NIL
Household Need	63%
What business can afford	35%
Only profit of the business	2%

The question in the survey relating to this aspect was, how do you decide or take decision, how much to take out of the business for your (personal) use ? It was hoped that respondents would describe how they calculate or the basis upon which they decide; how much the business could afford. However, according to the survey, the respondents were less detailed than was hoped. They showed (Table – 6.22) several different ways of taking drawing decisions. The responses were categorised into :

Salary - which means a fixed amount taken each week or month. Not a single respondent took salary from the business. As they feel, it is their own business, so salary or wages did not come into consideration.

Wage plus bonus - which means that a specific amount was taken out regularly and bonus were taken if justified by the profit. Here again no respondent took this option as their drawing decision.

Business afford ability - This covered all responses which indicated that drawing decision varied on a weekly basis depending on business activity. For example, one respondent said, "As this is my own business whatever is left after paying everything is mine." According to the survey result 35 p.c. of the respondents employed this option for their drawing.

House hold need - responses in this category indicated that they only took enough for basic living expenses. According to the survey result largest group i.e. 63 p.c. of the owner-managers of the small businesses of North-East Region, withdraw from the business on the basis of amount needed for house-hold expenses.

Net profit - very few small businesses under study, mostly partnership firms, opted for withdrawing money from the business after calculating business net profit for the year. Only 2 p.c. of the small businesses adopt this process of withdrawal.

Analysis of the features of the business :

Table 6.23
Drawing method employed by the small business.

	Age of the Business		Number of owner		Achievement	
Methods of Drawing	Less than 5(five) years (N – 67)	More than 5(five) years (N – 124)	One owner (N – 176)	More than one owner) (N-15)	Doing well (N – 109)	Not doing well (N – 82)
Salary	NIL	NIL	NIL	NIL	NIL	NIL
Wage+Bonus	NIL	NIL	NIL	NIL	NIL	NIL
House hold need	77.6%	55%	79%	6.7%	63%	65%
What business can afford	73%	47%	29%	60%	36%	35%
Profit of the business	NIL	3%	0.6%	33%	3.7%	-

Age of the business

Young businesses (less than 5 years of age) are considerably more likely to have taken only enough for their household requirement (nearly 78 p.c.). Older businesses (more than 5 years of age) on the other hand had divided almost equally between household needs (55 p.c.) and what business can afford (47 p.c.).

One owner and more than one owner

Small businesses with only one owner (sole proprietorship) show the highest (79 p.c.) tendency to draw out of the business and use that for meeting their household requirements. Firms with more than one owner (partnership firm) were more likely to take drawings depending on what business can afford (60 p.c.) and the profit of the business (33 p.c.). This would be a likely decision process in order to avoid the hassles of agreement on how much each owner should take out of the business.

Level of Achievement

There is no significant difference between firms doing well and not doing well with regard to drawing behaviour.

The data analysis and interpretation as presented above in Chapter -VI and also on the basis of other information collected from the respondents, the important findings are summarised in Chapter – VII next.

CHAPTER SEVEN

RESEARCH FINDINGS : A SUMMARY

From the present research, following observations are drawn about Financial Management Practices of small business units in North-Eastern region of India :

(1) The survey revealed that sole-proprietorships business consists of 92 p.c. of the respondent and 8 p.c. of thc sample units were partnership units. No co-operative and company form of business were found in the study.

(2) There is a predominance of small business activities in the retail trade sector (Nearly 70 p.c. of the oample units). It seems that, retailing activity is more attractive to the small businessman of this region than any other business activities. This is because of a stable demand for basic needs such as food and clothing which are mostly produced outside the region and also the need for a low level of skill/knowledge to start a retail business in small scale.

(3) Small business owner-managers are relatively young, 30-40 years of age account for nearly 61.76 p.c. of the sample units, which can be seen as a positive factor in terms of entrepreneurship and small business developed through self employment. Being young (within 40 years of age) they could be more receptive to further training and development to manage their businesses effectively and efficiently.

(4) The small business units do not realise the usefulness of financial management techniques. This is also because these units have limited resources – both financial and human – to spare for devising any sophisticated accounting system. The way they were maintaining their accounts and financial information, was satisfactory to them as according to owner-manager's perception nearly 86 p.c. of the respondent opined that they have no problem with financial management of their business units.

(5) Most of the respondent (89 p.c.) of the survey reported that they do not follow the double entry system of book keeping. What ever records (financial in nature) they (small businesses) maintained for day to day control and monitoring of business performance, were in the form of single entry system, conversion of which into double entry system were almost impossible.

(6) The record keeping system adopted by small business units are inadequate to provide support to financial management tools and techniques for analysis of the information. These businesses developed their own tailor-made accounting techniques which are informal and incomplete in nature, generally based on traditional 'Mahajani' system (Soral and Jain, 1994).

(7) Business performance appraisal through profit and loss account and Balance sheet (yearly) is one of the most important tool of financial management. But, the study revealed that only 24.6 p.c. of the sample units prepare profit and loss account and balance sheet yearly. They mostly prepares the annual accounts with the help of tax consultant for Income Tax purpose, which has very little relevance with actual business purposes.

(8) It was found that 51.3 p.c. of the small business assess their business performances of their units with sales volume, not through preparing profit and loss account for the business.

(9) As the awareness level of owner-manager was very poor, very few financial analysis tools and techniques were properly used by the respondent to assess the level of performance/achievement/growth of the business unit. In most of the cases, small business decision process is the result of 'experience', intuition or 'guess work'.

(10) It was revealed that 90 p.c. of the respondents did not keep their record of stock or inventory in a systematic manner through stock register or using any method of inventory management/control. They generally follow the physical verification of their stock at the end of the year.

(11) The owner managers of the small businesses under study knew the most important indicators needed for monitoring their businesses. As all the respondent (100 p.c.) said that even if they did not have firm figures or formal accounting records, but they knew (according to their own perception) how their business was doing. The study observed that small business owner-managers employed a multidimensional and non-quantitative decision process which were primarily informal in nature. This was corroborated by Rice and Hamiltan, (1979) study.

(12) With regard to pricing, all the small business units/firms have at least one method of establishing or calculating price of their product or services and some had used two methods. In general, full cost + p.c. of profit and purchase price + p.c. of profit are the most popular methods.

This process appeared to be better understood by the small business owner-managers than anticipated. Although, the sample units used these methods of pricing not on pen or paper but on the idea (presence of mind and experience) no formalised methods were employed in actual practices. They only make rough estimation of unit costs. Therefore, firms were unsure whether the price they were also charging was correct or not, as they were also not sure of the effects on demand of a change in price.

(13) In setting prices of their products/services, the study observed some significant difference between different sector of the small businesses in North-Eastern region of India (according to Chi-square test). Majority of the manufacturing units (68 p.c.) use full cost + p.c. of profit, service units adopt full cost (48.6 p.c.) and market price (28.5 p.c.). On the other hand, retailers mostly use either full cost + p.c. of profit (61 p.c.) or purchase price + p.c. of profit (34 p.c.).

(14) Based on the perspective literature the expectation was that comprehensive financial reporting and financial analysis, generally lead to improved financial control and that this in itself could significantly increase the chances of a small business prospering (survival) through growth. On the other hand, given the complex dynamics of small business growth, it may be unrealistic to expect that only superior and proper financial management and analysis practices with appropriate financial tools and techniques will stand out as correlates with success. Non-parametric test (Chi-squire test) of the associations between the financial reporting and analysis variables and the means of financial performance (Doing well/not doing well) as perceived by the owner manager failed to provide much additional evidence of significant relationships. As the finding of this study and earlier studies have shown, such a direct causal link was difficult to establish. Thomas and Evanson (1987), McMahon and Davies (1994), Nayak and Greenfield (1994) were similarly unable to establish such relationships.

Yet, it does show that firms doing well were most likely to have good knowledge and detailed record keeping process for the business.

(15) No method of analysis were followed by the sample business units, while making their capital investment decision. Their capital investment decision were based on Necessity – 51.3 p.c.; Efficiency – 39.8 p.c.; Bank Finance – 8.9 p.c. Therefore, it observed by the study that no method of appraisal were followed in making capital investment decision. Observation, was the most important aspects of capital expenditure decision. There were no significant difference between young/old business, or the experience/in experience owner-managers of small businesses.

(16) It was observed that only 10.47 p.c. of the small business units used computer in monitoring their accounting records. While analysing the data it was found that only 11.36 p.c. of the trading units, 11.4 p.c. of the service sector and only 4.5 p.c. in manufacturing sector used computer. This results compares almost exactly with Brooksbank et. al., (1992) and when compared with those of Griffiths and Dorsman (1987) and Chen and Williams, (1993) and surprisingly indicates that size of business (in terms of sales turnover) is a key factor in deciding to put accounting records on computer.

(17) The survey revealed that only 15 p.c. of the business units prepare their records or makes their financial data uptodate daily. Another 36 p.c. monthly and 49 p.c. prepare their accounts yearly.

(18) None of the sample units could make difference between private assets and expenses with their business assets and expenses. As they feel that it is their own business therefore separation between business and personal expenses – is of no used.

(19) Not a single unit prepare cash flow and fund flow statement for their business to know the fund position of the business in a particular period of time.

(20) The study observed that 98.4 p.c. of the respondents used to allow deferred payments to their customer.

(21) For credit sale, all of the respondents generally allow credit to their customer through open account i.e. without following any credit policy. As no systematic credit policy were followed by the small business units therefore, the credit worthiness of the customers is not taken into consideration. Past business experience was considered to be the only risk assessment technique used to evaluate the credit worthiness of a person.

(22) No respondent make provision for bad and doubtful debt.

(23) No reserve fund was created by the small business units from their yearly profit.

(24) No financial ratios were used to analyse the financial statement.

(25) In case of costing it was found that nearly 98.4 p.c. of the respondents could not able to separate direct or indirect cost of production. It was also surprising that 96 p.c. of the manufacturing units were unable to separate their direct and indirect costs which is one of the most important factor in price fixation of a product for sale in a competitive market environment.

(26) Regarding fixed and variable cost not a single unit could split the cost between this two variables.

(27) It was observed that only 5.8 p.c. of the small business units gets their accounts audited by the qualified auditor. It was also found that most of the (big) small business in terms of sales turnover were employed qualified auditor (firms) to audit their accounts annually.

(28) Regarding drawing decision from the business by the owner manager it was found that 63 p.c. withdraw from the business for house hold needs, 35 p.c. withdraw from business according to what business can afford and only 2 p.c. withdraw only profit from the business.

(29) Small business in this region used bank finance as one of the most important source of finance. As nearly

45 p.c. of the small business units received bank loan for the business. Hire purchase system is not popular method of financing (only 2 p.c.). No other form of financing like Leasing, venture capital, equity capital was observed. Although internal sources like retirement of profit, bringing new capital and initial capital by the owner manager from the own sources which were continue to be one of the main source of finance for their small businesses of this region.

(30) While assessing the performance level and frequency of preparing financial records it was found that 10 p.c. of the respondents who prepare daily their financial records were doing well in their respective businesses.

(31) The analysis give interesting feature about the different types of business, retail traders who have the least complex decision process seemed the most diligent record keeper as 92 p.c. of them keeps their account themselves and all of them maintain cash book, debtors book and creditors book. Level of awareness was also high among the retail business units owner/manager compare to manufacturing and service units.

(32) There are several problems of Internal Management dislocating the general progress of small business units. Some of these problem were discovered under this study were as follows :

- Most of these small business units are grown by individual promoters. They come with personal egos and ideas, proprietorial attitudes and ineffective delegation. In short it's a one man show.
- The progress of an organisation depends heavily on mindset, courage and vision of the owner manager. This is at times influenced by personal and family requirement.
- The organisation structure is not built, targets and budgets are not worked out. The systems and procedures are not defined or transparent. Planning is not corporated and dealing are informal.

- The owner-managers of small businesses are lack of professional expertise, with out much of real accountability to outside agency.
- In many instances, business ideas and exposures are not upto date and adequate, rules and regulations are less understood, product and market knowledge are not upto the mark, business remains confined within local or regional market.

(33) The recommended way to plan and monitor a business's activities is through the use of a budget. Deviation between budget and actual performance will enable the owner-manager to change his actions to get back on course. It was felt that, with regard to small businesses which were being studied, not a single unit prepare budget but would tend to use previous experiences as an adhoc budget.

(34) Due to maximum involvement of the owner-managers (proprietors) in all aspects of decision making in these small businesses, much of the information they need is picked up intuitively and formal records were not used much on a day-to-day basis.

(35) It was discovered from the study that, bigger units of small businesses (more than one owner-manager and monthly sales turnover is more than Rs. one lakh) kept more records and also knew more about their business units.

(36) The results of the study show that there is a big gap between theory and practice of financial management tools and techniques as reported. The survey result also revealed the fact. Awareness level of owner-manager of financial management tools and techniques of record keeping and analysis were very poor. It seems small business owner-managers were running into business without proper financial management know-how.

(37) It was readily apparent from the data that multi-factor

considerations were an important factor/aspect of small business owner-managers decision making processes. Due to the size of the business, the owner-manager was fully involved in the day-to-day operation of the firm. Therefore, he was likely to be involved in all levels of decision making. A major complication arises in the fact that the small business owner-manager will be forced to deal with a wide variety of decision area's simultaneously. Therefore, considering his extremely broad decision responsibility and the necessity of dealing with highly varied and concurrent decisions, the owner-manager of small business was forced to sharply limit the depth of his analysis in all areas. Here to support the findings, it is revealed by the research that small businesses did not use any techniques of budgeting analysis or forecasting to take informed and judged decision by the owner-manager.

(38) The small businesses has vast sources of information related to business, generating during the business. Unfortunately, as suggested by Simon (1955), the owner-manager has only a finite ability to process this information. Very often the small business owner-managers take his decision on some poorly defined interaction of the factors he chooses to consider.

(39) As in most of the cases owner-manager's decision making process was more difficult as he rarely has any mechanisms for filtering or comparing or analysing the information impinging on him from various inputs which was not properly recorded according to the prudent financial management terms. He (owner-manager) then perceives this information as Cleland (1960) suggests as unorganised, distorted and full of irrelevant 'noise'. Thus the owner-managers of small business often has great difficulty in synthesizing an optional solution to what ever problem that faces the firm. These may be the most important drawback for a small business management, which can affect the

firm's sustenance. Many of these owner-managers stated that a majority of their decisions were the result of 'experience', 'intuition' or 'guess work'. This implies that there was no decision process involved which intern shows that small businesses under study utilised primarily a very informal approach to decision-making.

(40) No systematic pricing of materials/goods/services is done. Application of marginal costing and standard costing are not at all observed.

(41) While most of the respondents are not aware of many important financial management tools and techniques and its usefulness, they opined that such a technique is hardly of any use for them. This way, most of the respondent (98 p.c.) were satisfied with whatever financial management practices they adopt.

(42) The results shows that the small businesses using a computer were large enough to have employees and were either in the retail trade (wholeseller) or in service activity. The proprietors (owner-managers) who had made the decision to obtain a computer were more likely to have ambitious business goals.

(43) The study discovered that, small businesses are less organised in their record-keeping does not necessarily indicate a lack of organisation and effectiveness, but may be due to a lack of perceived requirement.

(44) The present study disclosed that the age of the businesses and their perceived level of achievement has no relationship (according to Chi-square test). They are independent.

(45) There is some relationship between different business sector (manufacturing/retail/service) and their level of achievement (according to Chi-square test). As it was observed that percentage of achievement level of service and retail trading units were good (doing well) compared to manufacturing units.

(46) Chi-square test revealed that there are some close relationship between size (according to monthly sales turnover) and the corresponding age of the business units. It was observed that big among the small business in terms of sales turnover, were older firms (more than 5 years of age).

(47) One of the major disclosure of the study is that business experience of the owner-managers of the small businesses has no significant relationship with their level of achievement/performances (Chi-square test).

(48) The present study draw the conclusion (with the help of Chi-square test) that the level of performance/achievement of the small businesses and frequency of record keeping has no relationship, they are independent. But on the other hand, age of the business unit and their frequency of record keeping has some relationship. Older (more than 5 years old) businesses were more particular and frequent in record keeping than the young businesses (less than 5 years old).

(49) The study finding highlighted the fact that there is no significant difference in the use of financial management tools and techniques between highly educated and less educated owner-manager of small businesses (Chi-square test result).

(50) It was discovered from the study that, more financial tools were used/practised, when the firm (small business) increases its size (according to monthly sales turnover).

(51) Various analysis in the study show that smaller younger firms in term of size (monthly sales turnover) and age (less than 5 years old) were managing with less records and knowledge than larger and older firm. This may be contributing to their lack of achievement. If the younger and smaller firms wish to grow they will need to develop more records and methods of information gathering.

(52) Capital expenditure decision show differences between young (less than 5 years old) and smaller firms (according to monthly sales turnover) compare to older and larger units. The smaller and younger firms tended to focus on necessity (72 p.c.), while older (more than 5 years old) and larger firms were more likely to use efficiency (57 p.c.) criterion for capital expenditure.

(53) Drawing decision of the owner-managers of the small businesses show some differences between young (less than 5 years old) and older (more than 5 years old) business units. As 78 p.c. of the younger business, withdraw from business for their household needs/ requirement. Older (more than 5 years old) business units on the other hand were divided between household needs (55 p.c.) and what business can afford (45 p.c.).

Single owner firms (sole proprietorship) show the most common tendency to take away from the business for meeting their household needs (79 p.c.).

CHAPTER EIGHT
SUGGESTIONS AND CONCLUSION

The changing economic circumstances have pushed our economy from "infant protection strategy" to the stage of economic liberalisation to meet the challenges of globalisation. Under these circumstances, it is but natural that the government is shifting its focus in terms of incentives and concessions to small scale industry by curtailing the fiscal concessions and other benefits doled out to this sector in 70's and 80's. This new but non-protective culture for small businesses, a different outlook with a competitive attitude to mobilising and utilising the resources, is needed by the small enterpreneurs in their struggle for existence in the age of 'survival of the fittest'.

Financial recording system adopted by the small business should be according to their requirement on the basis of prudent accounting norms and easy to follow, so that it can provide foundation for financial management applications in small business.

➢ The result of the study highlights the wide gap between theory and practice of financial management in small business organisation's. Small Business owner-managers may hardly find the existing financial management techniques of use. At the same time, little efforts has been made in the field of research on developing tools and techniques for small business (Soral and Jain, 1994). With their peculiar problems and limited resources, this small business sector generally "relies more on traditional accounting namely financial and taxation matters, rather than financial management. The theories of financial management, so far developed, has little relevance in catering to the specific needs of the small business. Thus, the theory and the practice of financial management being interdependent may form a vicious circle hindering the growth of this vital sector. In this age of cut-throat competition, more sophisticated financial management tools cannot be a luxury for small business units to flourish. However the onus of designing suitable kit for financial management for small business lies on the academics, which in turn calls for the need of a "real life research" (Choudhury, 1987).

- Review of the effectiveness and uses of the management thought, in most of the previous analyses is recorded in the context of large corporate sectors. But if we want to unearth the correct perspective, it is observed that only 500, out of 5,00,000 active business enterprises are recognised corporate setups. Ironically, more than 90 per cent of our industrial units, with turnover in the range of a few thousand, continue to function in an apparently, unprofessional way. So any isolated attempt to improve the efficiency of these few giants may be futile, without improving the rest of the business sector. Following the examples of ASEAN tigers, we must concentrate on the medium and small scale business enterprises, for all round development including financial management aspect. A separate Ministry/Department at the centre and in the states level may be created to formulate appropriate policy measures for development of small business administration covering small trading, manufacturing and all other types of small businesses in the line of USA, UK, Japan etc..
- The management techniques initially most valuable to

the small business are apparently those which will enable it to conserve its financial resources in liquid form. Prudent and skilful purchasing and pricing, careful planning and control of expenditure of all kinds, proper maintenance of inventory without interrupting production, expanding work through the shops to avoid accumulating work-in-progress, standardisation of its products or services are of immense value to any business firm. They are vital to the small business wishing to maintain some financial freedom of action.

- At the present stage, it is sad to observe that young technical manpower is shifting to white collar and office jobs, instead of being groomed in factory shop floors. As a result, the think tank of our industries are starved of essential tech-force nourishment and the outcome is self restraining. On the other hand, our management curriculum has not really looked into the requirements of these medium and small scale sector of businesses. Also, trained managers are rarely interested in working for this sector and generally do not understand or contribute, even if capacitated. Largely, the scope of professionalism does not get an entry in small business sector.
- To cope up the situation few action plans may be taken up for urgent implementation. First, is to devise effective low cost management training programmes, particularly suitable for small business sectors/industries, and thereby groom young competent managers for their future involvement in this sector. Even tailor made in plant training courses may be organised. Exposure should be carefully designed to impart beneficial working. Second, is to facilitate low cost turnkey total management consultation, to be offered from sincere, like-minded, experienced professionals. This consultancy services can also be provided by professional management schools, universities and technical

institutions, through setting up of 'Management Consultancy Wings' at the institutional level.

- The small business survival planning requires well thought out strategies by the entrepreneurs regarding the following crucial and challenging aspects :

Finance : Lack of adequate and timely finance has been rated as the foremost problem of the Small Businesses. The problem is of both working capital funds and long term loans. The sector is in dire need of term capital in order to upgrade and for modernisation. To meet this challenge a proper fund management programme through financial management practices with a cost conscious approach is required by the small business entrepreneurs. Temptation to divert the fund to unrelated activities should be avoided.

Locational advantage : Small business units cater generally to small geographical areas and they are in a rather better position to find opportunities suitable for the local people and market. Therefore, instead of scattering their efforts over large market areas, they can put concentrated efforts in defined areas.

Marketing : This has been identified as an important problem area affecting the growth of the sector by many research studies. The competitive marketing attributes like packaging, branding, distribution network storage, design, technology, promotion, quality control and after sales services are beyond the reach of small scale businesses. But with growing competition, the sector would need to strengthen its marketing system in order to survive and grow.

Due to their modest investment in plant and machinery and small level of output, small units are more adaptable to the dynamic condition of the market place. Further, small units can tap the market of specialised (niche) products even if the total volume of demand is not very significant. In service sector satisfaction of the consumer to a large extent is dependent upon the personal attention paid to him. Small firms generally are in a better position to provide the personal touch so important for success in service industries. There are perishable products like bread, and other edibles which require extremely fast and efficient distribution system. Local small business units can get much better penetration into the market in such cases. Small entrepreneurs should, therefore, identify their major strengths and try to convert them into market opportunities.

- Timely and correct information has a significant place in a business. Generally, it is found that small business organisations are giving less attention to collecting proper information relating to various business activities in time. Lack of proper and timely information creates a serious problem before an entrepreneur in shaping ideas and proper planning. To sustain in a competitive field of activities, a serious effort is needed for collection and analysis of latest information (financial and non-financial) for long term planning for the organisation.
- An accounting system which is the basis of financial management as all the financial data is first of all recorded according to the rules of accounting in the business books of accounts. The accounting system is only useful for financial management if it is upto date and accurate. To prevent errors and to provide correct information of the business, the business accounting system must provide for certain internal checks. A standard method for protecting against errors or employee fraud is to have two or more individuals involved in the recording function. An alternative approach for ensuring accuracy is to employ the services of a public accountant or a book-keeper. Assistance may also be provided by a book-keeping service firm in filling out tax returns and in making periodic audits. Still another approach to handling the accounting function is to purchase one of a number of simplified book-keeping systems (software) that have been prepared for use by small business. Such systems are ideal for the business owner who knows

little about accounting and has some workable knowledge on computer.

- The present study, have identified few tools of modern financial management, which are very useful for the management of a business successfully. But there is no denying the fact that small business units in North Eastern Region of India including Assam are facing some problems, which makes the application of these tools difficult due to lack of knowledge, awareness and usefulness of the tools as most of the firm are marginal units. Difficulties are there, but they are not insurmountable, given the determination and concerted efforts – problems of implementation can be overcomed. There is no short cut to success in financial management. There is no alternative to the observance of proper discipline and financial ethics for ensuring the optimal and efficient use of financial resources like Capital for a business. Therefore, all-out efforts are needed for applying the tools of financial management to the small business enterprises in a simplified and scientific manner in the interest of injecting fresh confidence and restoring the financial health of the organisation in particular and the nation as a whole.
- Small Business enterprises play a critical role in the development and growth of local and regional economies by creating employment and commercialising innovations that result in economic growth. Development factors for small enterprises include sources of innovations, opportunities for new products and/or services within defined market places and a supportive public and private infrastructure. It is through systematic direction of technical support and assistance that indigenous small-businesses can prosper.

Owner-managers of small businesses admit the usefulness of modern techniques of financial management, but express disappointment over the benefit from their application due to ignorance. Although, the owner-manager of the small business units under study has shown some interest in modern techniques of financial management, yet they are not mentally prepared to adopt these tools. This is in many cases due to their inadequate knowledge of the subject inadequate manpower, insufficient practices of these tools by other organisation in the same line of business and so on. Therefore, the present attitude of the owner-manager of small business has to be changed and attempt should be made to develop a positive attitude towards the use of financial management tools. For this, measures should be taken to familiarise the owner-managers with modern tools, and their benefits to be derived from their use etc. through the provision of training, short term courses, conferences, seminars/workshops etc. by the development agencies.

- The present system of education in India, where pigeonholes individuals into a narrow range of disciplines and straightjackets them into rigid career tracks. Given the overwhelming emphasis on grades, creativity and independent thinking end up taking a back seat. Therefore, the need of the hour is an education system that foster exploration, questioning and debate. A system that can help each student/individual to pursue a path that best stimulates their creativity and to face challenges by him or her to become successful entrepreneur. The objective should be to create citizens who have the ability to think laterally.
- As we understand, the present small business definition in India was framed to withstand the competition from the large scale industries within the country, in a protective environment of 60's and 70's. But at present Indian economy has underwent a 'U' turn from protection to a market economy where we need a broad based small business definition to withstand the competition. In the proposed new definition, where limits on investment have to be removed and include all the constituent of small business i.e. Trade, Industry and Commerce to meet the present challenges. Therefore, government policies

have to shift its direction from investment criteria to employment in defining small business. The proposed shift in the policy shall act as a facilitator of economic activities – as small business may be promoted in the light of employment generation and to cultivate the spirit of entrepreneurship in the country's economy.

➢ The result of the study shows that only 10.5% of the small businesses uses computer. At the level of the small business obtaining computer for book-keeping and financial management purposes for many such businesses is almost certainly not cost effective. However, many other businesses especially those who are using computers are discovering the advantages of computer use for many purposes other than financial management and accounting, e.g. word processing, desk-top publishing, work schedules, stock records, etc. which change the equation by not only just saving on time or personnel but also making the business more professional and efficient. Therefore, it may be suggested that most small business owner-managers need more management training in computer literacy and use of computers for accounting, pricing and budgeting, office management etc. If more owner-managers are to feel confident enough to use the technology it may be that support systems need to be made available to help inexperienced users to deal with day to day problems which arise when using computer software and tools of financial management. This could be provided either through help-lines to suppliers or through appropriate local networking.

➢ The result of the study support the conclusion that receivable management in Small Businesses requires an urgent attention. Following a liberal credit policy will tend to increase in sales and also lead to an increase in account receivable. Consequently, small firms shall require more financial resources to continue the existing level of business activities. The seriousness of the receivable problem is emphasised by the aggregate losses on bad-debt (lost sales) incurred; most conservative estimate run into lakhs of rupees every year (Das and Dey, 2004). The longer a credit sale is carried on the book, the greater is the likelihood of its not being collected in full. The losses on bad-debts show the necessity of close follow-up on accounts which become part-due.

Therefore, the best way to avoid receivable problems is to avoid giving credit in the first place. It is said that, no sale, however large, is worth making if you cannot collect receivable in time. So, management must adopt judicious decision and cautious approach for granting credit.

Small Businesses should adopt a reasonable and tough credit policy. A sound credit policy is one in which :

(a) Limits are placed in the amount of credit to be extended.

(b) Terms of credit sales clearly specified.

(c) Receivables are systematically monitored and controlled.

(d) Followup action on delinquent account receivable should be taken up promptly.

(e) Aggressive collection procedure, should be initiated.

(f) Delivery of goods or services on credit should not be made until the previous balance of receivable has actually been cleared - if any.

- So to increase the awareness level of Small Business owner/managers about accounting, record keeping and financial control, a concerted effort must be taken up by the Small Business development authorities like, DIC, SISI, SIDBI, Commercial Banks through EDP's.
- In conclusion, this study's major findings will hopefully help focus the attention of researchers, business practitioners and policy makers on the needs and challenges facing small businesses. These small

business units/firms can be formidable competitive forces both domestically and internationally, as they often are the sources of technological innovation and employment generation for developing country like India. Such findings should accelerate the search for ways to improve the capacity of small firms to match their high growth rates in sales with higher profitability levels.

Recommendation for Further Research

(a) It must be noted that since our study was confined to situations at a particular point in time. The survey data could not explain what Financial Management practices in Small Businesses in North East India have changed over time. In certain period of time, however, some of these practices may have been different from those revealed by our study. Therefore, further research is needed to examine what financial management practices in North-East Region of India have changed in the recent past and in what direction they are moving at present.

(b) Due to the exploratory nature of the study and limited scope, there remains considerable opportunity for further empirical inquiry into the small businesses financial management functions and practices. The researcher believe that it would be useful to extend this study into a wider empirical effort by developing a broader and more specified questionnaire and covering other parts of the country. This would be an important step for determining whether the relationships and findings identified in this study exist in other small enterprises. The results of such studies could, in turn, generate theories and research questions for more general testing and research.

(c) Decision behaviour of owner-managers of small businesses is largely the result of habit and experience. Further research should focus on techniques and ways to train entrepreneurs (owner-mangers) to be more comprehensive in decision making. Such efforts are likely to result in increases in business performances.

(d) Other issues in the small enterprise Financial Management objective function which might require investigation include the longitudinal analysis of how the transferability of ownership stakes affects the financial management of small businesses. The variation of the financial management practices between different kinds of small business units might require investigation.

(e) Within the limitations of the study the findings give some support to the proposition that small business financial management practices is not underpinned by wealth-maximizing assumptions alone. While, this conclusion cannot be generalised to the wider small enterprise population, the findings of the study are consistent with relevant literature and support the need for further research.

(f) Finally, there is a need to replicate our findings using different populations and measures and larger samples. For example, different measures of performance should be employed, firms in other regions of the country should be surveyed and larger sample sizes should be analysed. In addition, future extensions of this research should give thought to including medium sized firms. Finally, a comparison of Indian small business firms with their counterparts in other countries would be a fruitful future research avenue.

BIBLIOGRAPHY

Abdul Khalik, A.R. and Ajinkya, B.B. (1979). "Empircal Research in Accounting : A Methodological Approach." *American Accounting Association* (AAA), New York.

Ambhore, G.M., Singh D.K. and Khushu, L.J. (1997). "Small Enterprise Management Techniques and Methodologies in U.K. : Quality Control." *SEDME* Vol. XXIV No. 1. March.

Anderson, D. (1982). "Small Industry in Developing Countries : A Discussion of Issues". *World Development*, 10(11), 913-948.

Ang, J.S. (1991). "Small Business Uniqueness and the Theory of Financial Management". *The Journal of Small Business Finance* 1(1), 1-13.

Aram, J.D. and Crowen, S.S. (1990). "Strategic Planning for Increased Profit in the Family Owned Business". *Long Range Planning*, December.

Baisya, P. (1986). "Role of Small Scale and Cottage Industries : A case study on Kamrup District, Assam". Ph.D. Thesis (unpublished), Gauhati University.

Bala, Shashi (1988). *Management of Small Scale Industries*. Deep and Deep Publication, New Delhi.

Barooah, H.K. (1980). "Prospect and Problems of Small Scale Industries in Lakhimpur District". Ph.D. Thesis (unpublished), Gauhati University.

Barpujari, Basanta, Kumar (2002). "Development of SSI's

and its socio-economic implication". The Sentinel, Monday, 28th January.

Barrow, C. (1988). *Financial Management for the Small Business.* (2nd edition) Kagan Page, London.

Barrow, Colin (1997). *The Essence of Small Business.* Prentice Hall, New Delhi. 1-17.

Baumback, Clifford, M. (1998). *How to organise and operate A Small Business.* Prentice Hall, USA. Pp. 1-11.

Bhattacharjee, P.R. (1998). "Relative Conributions of Economic and Non-Economic factors to industrial backwardness of the North-Eastern region".

Biswal, N.B., Baidya, D., Kumar, Anil and Suryanarayana, Hema (1997). "Supporting Small Business Development: A comparison between the approaches of United Kingdom and India". *SEDME,* Vol. XXIV. No. 2. June.

Black, Nelms (1950). *How to organize and manage a Small Business.* University of Oklahoma Press, USA.

Bolton Committee (1971). *Small Firms – Report of the Committee of Inquiry on Small Firms.* London : HMSO, U.K.

Borland, C. (1974). *Locus of Control, Need for Achievement and Entrepreneurship.* (Doctoral Dissertation, University of Taxas).

Boyer, P. and Roth, H. (1978). "The cost of Equity Capital for Small Business". *American Journal of Small Business* 2(1), 1-11.

Bracker, J.S. and Pearson, J.N. (1986). "Planning and Financial Performance of Small, Mature Firms". *Strategic Management Journal* (Nov. – Dec.) 503-522, U.S.A.

Bracker, J.S., Keats, B.W. and Pearson, J.N. (1988). "Planning and Financial Performance among small firm in a Growth Industry" *Strategic Management Journal*, Nov.-Dec., pp. 591-603.

Branch, S. (1991). *A Good Plan Is Key to Business Success.* Black Enterprise, November, pp. 68-70.

Brigham, E.F. and Smith, K.V. (1967). "Cost of Capital to the Small Firm". *The Engineering Economist* (Fall), 1-26.

Brokaw, L. (1992). *The Secret of Great Planning.* Inc., October. pp. 151-157.

Brooksbank, R.; Kirby, D. and Kane, S. (1992). "IT Adoption and The Independent Retail Business : The Retail Newsagency". *International Small Business Journal*, April-June. Vol. 10. No. 3, 53-61.

Buckland, Roger and Davis, Edward. W. (ed) (1995). *Finance for Growing Enterprises.* Routledge, U.K.

Burton, James, E. and Hillison, William (1979). "Big GAAP Little GAAP : Is Accounting for Small Business in the balance?". *American Journal of Small Business.* Vol. III. No. 3. January.

Carran, James and Blackburn, Robert. A. (ed) (1991). Paths of Enterprise – the future of the Small Business. Routledge, U.K. (1991).

Carsberg, B.V. and Edey, H.C. (1969). *Modern Financial Management.* (Edt). Penguin Books Ltd. U.K.

Chatterjee, B.K. (1999). *Finance for Non-Finance Managers.* Jaico Publishing House, New Delhi.

Chen, J.C. and William, B. (1993). "The Impact of Microcomputer Systems on Small Businesses : England, 10 years Later". *Journal of Small Business Management* (July), 96-102.

Choudhuri, P.R. (1998). "Capital Structure Planning in Small Scale Industries". *Finance India.* Vol. XII, No. 1, March, 1998, 21-32.

Chowdhury, M. Shamsul Haque (1995). "Small Business in Bangladesh : What we need to make it". *SEDME.* Vol – XII No. 3 Sept.

Chuta, E. and Liedholm, C. (1975). *The role of Small Scale Industries in Employment Generation and Rural Development.* Michigan State University, Department of Agricultural Economics.

Cochram, A.B. (1981). "Small Business Mortality Rates – A Review of the Literature". *Journal of Small Business Management* 19 (4). 50-59.

Colley, Philip, L. (1992). *Business Financial Management.* (3rd Edition) The Dryden Press, USA.

Cooley, P.L. and Edwards C.E. (1983). "Financial Objectives of Small Firms". *American Journal of Small Business* 8(1), 27-31.

Crook, Nigel (1993). *Indian Industrial Cities – Essays in Economy and Demography.* Oxford University Press, Delhi.

D' Amboise, G. and Gasse, Y. (1980). *Performance in Small Firms and the Utilization of Formal Management Techniques* paper presented to the Joint National Meeting of the Institute of Management Science and Operations Research Society of America, Washington, D.C.

Danziger, S.H. and Weinberg, D.H. (1986). *Fighting Poverty : What works and What does not.* Cambridge : Harvard University Press.

Das, Ashim Kumar (1998). "Financing of Small Scale Sector (A study of Cachar district of Assam)". M.Phil. Dissertation (Unpublished), Assam University, Silchar.

Das, Ashim Kumar and Dey, Nikhil Bhusan (2003). "Conceptualisation of Small Business in India : An Analytical Study". *SEDME,* Hyderabad. Vol. 30. No. 2. June.

Das, Ashim Kumar and Dey, Nikhil Bhusan (2004). "Effective Management of Receivables in Small Business". *SEDME,* Hyderabad, Vol. 31. No. 1. March.

Das, K.R.; Sinha, K.M.; Palchoudhury, K.S.; Yadav, H.N. (1999). *Theory and Practice of Book-keeping and Accountancy* (Part-II). Lawyer's Book Stall, Guwahati. pp. 1-19.

Datta Roy, B. and Baishya, Prabin (1998). *Sociological Constraints to Industrial Development in North-East India* (Ed.), Concept Publishing Company, New Delhi.

Deb, Ranabijoy (1993). *Small Scale Industries in India (Case study from Assam).* Mittal Publication, New Delhi.

Dewhurst, Jim and Burns, Paul (1983). *Small Business Finance and Control.* The MacMillan Press, London, U.K.

Dewhurst, Jim and Burns, Paul (1993). *Small Business Management* (3rd Edition). The MacMillan Press Ltd., U.K.

Dey N.B. (1980). "Small Scale Industries in Cachar District : Their growth problems and prospects". Ph.D. Thesis (unpublished), Gauhati University, Guwahati.

Dhameja, Nand and Sastry, K.S. (1998). *Finance and Accounting for managerial competitiveness.* Wheeler Publishing, New Delhi.

Drucker, Peter (1954). *The Practice of Management.* Harper and Row, New York.

Dunne, P.M.; Ezell, D.E. and Roberts, A.T. (1980). "The use of Accounting Information in the Small Business firm's Planning and Control Process". *American Journal of Small Business.* Vol. IV, No. 4, Spring (April-June).

Dunne, Patrick. M., Ezell, Dee. E. and Roberts, Arthur. T. (1980). "The use of Accounting Information In the Small Business Firm's Planning and Control Process." *American Journal of Small Business,* USA. Vol. IV. No. 4 Spring (April – June).

Dutt, Ruddar (1999). "Role of SSE in Socio-Economic Perspective". *IASSI,* Vol. 18. No. I.

Ezra, Solomon (1969). *The Theory of Financial Management.* Columbia University Press. U.S.A.

Fayol, Henri (1949). *General and Industrial Management.* Pitman Publishing, New York.

Fehh, Arthur, M. (1981). "A profile of the Small Business Sector in France". *American Journal of Small Business.* Vol. VI, No. 2 (Oct.-Dec.), U.S.A.

Fredrickson, J.W. and Mitchell, T.R. (1984). "Strategic decision processes : Comprehensiveness and performance in a unstable industry". *Academy of Management Journal*, 27(2) : pp. 399-423.

Gibb, A. and Terry, W. (1980). *Policy issues in Small Business Research*. Teakfield Limited, U.K.

Grablowsky, B.J. and William, L.B. (1980). "The Application of Capital Allocation Techniques by Small Business". *Journal of Small Business Management*, Vol. 18, No. 3. USA.

Greenwood, William. T. (1967). *Business Policy : A Management Audit Approach*. The MacMillan Company, New York. pp. 23-24.

Griffith, J; Dorsman, M. (1987). "SMEs New Technology and Training". *International Small Business Journal*. Vol. 5 (Spring), 30-42.

Hamilton, R. (1987). "Motivation and Aspirations of Business Founders". *International Small Business Journal* 6(1), 70-78.

Hankinson, A. (1977). "The Investment Behaviour of the Smaller Manufacturing Business Unit in the Plymouth Area 1970-1975". Ph.D. Thesis, University of Bath, USA.

Harmon, Paul (1979). *Small Business Management - A Practical Approach*. D. Van Nostrand Company, New York. USA.

Harper, Malcolm (1984). *Small Business in the Third World : Guideline for Practical Assistance*. New York, John Wiley.

Hill, Terry (1991). *Small Business Production/Operation Management*. Macmillan Education Ltd., U.K.

Hillidge, J. (1990). *Planning for Growth in a Small Company*. Long Range Planning. June, pp. 76-81.

Holmes, S. (1986). "The Practising Accountant, Accounting Information and Small Business". Small Business Review, *AGPS*, Canberra.

Holmes, S. (1986). "The Practising Accountant, Accounting Information and small business". Small Business Review, *AGPS*, Canberra.

Holmes, S. and Nicholls, D. (1989). "Modelling the Accounting Information requirement of Small Business". *Accounting and Business Research*, USA.

Holmes, Scott and Nicholls, Des. (1988). "An Analysis of the use of Accounting information by Australian Small Business." *Journal of Small Business Management*, USA. April.

Horne, James, C. and Wachowicz, John, M. (Jr.) (1996). *Fundamentals of Financial Management.* Prentice Hall of India (P) Ltd., New Delhi.

Hughes, A. and Storey, D.J. (ed) (1994). *Finance and the Small Firm.* Rautledge, U.K.

Hutchinson, P. and Ray, G. (1986). *Surviving the Financial Stress of Small Enterprise Growth – in the survival of Small Firm.* Vol. I "The Economics of Survival and Entrepreneurship" ed. J. Curran, J. Stanworth and D. Watkins, Aldershot, Gower, 53-71.

International Labour Organisation (1990). "The Promotion of Self-employment". *Proceedings of International Labour Conference*, 77th Session, Geneva, 1990.

International Labour Organisation (1992). *Small Enterprise Development Programme – Integrated Strategies for Small Enterprise Development.* A Policy Paper. Geneva, Switzerland : ILO.

James, E. and Rose Ackerman, S. (1986). *Non profit Enterprise in Market Economics.* New York : Starwood Academic Publications.

Janis, I.L., and Mann, L. (1977). *Decision-Making.* Free Press, New York.

Jones, D.W. (1982). "Characteristics of Planning in Small Firms". *Journal of Family Owned Business Management* (July), 15-25.

Jones, T. Colwyn. (1995). *Accounting and the Enterprise (A Social Analysis).* Rutledge. U.K.

Karlson, C., Johannisson, B. and Storey, D. (1993). *Small Business Dynamics* Ed. Routledge, U.K.

Kashyap, S.P. (1995). *Emerging Industrial Policy Reforms : Implication for Small Size Enterprises.* Productivity. April-June, Vol. 36, No. 1.

Keasey, Kevin and Watson, Robert (1993). *Small firm management ownership, finance and performance.* Blackwell Publishers, U.K.

Keats, B. and Bracker, J. (1988). "Toward a Theory of Small Firm Performance : A Conceptual Model". *American Journal of Small Business* (Spring) 41-58.

Knapp, Michael. C. (1994). *Financial Accounting* (Issues and Cases)". West Publishing Company, USA.

Knight, R.A. (1993). "Planning : The key to Family – Owned Business Survival". *Management Accounting.* February. pp. 33-34.

Konstans, C. and R.P. Martin (1982). "Financial Analysis for Small Business : A Model for Control". *Business.* Vol. 32. 21-26.

Kothari, C.R. (1996). *Research Methodology : Methods and Techniques.* Wishwa Prakashan, New Delhi.

Kristof, N.D. (1985). *The Third World : Back to the Farm.* New York Times, 28th July.

Kuchl, Charles, R. and Lambing, Peggy. (1994). *Small Business Planning and Management.* The Dryden Press, USA.

Kuratko, Donald, F.; Hornsby, Jeffrey, S. and Naffziger, Douglas, W. (1996). "An Examination of Owner's Goals in Sustaining Enterpreneurship". *Journal of Small Business Management,* U.S.A.

Kyambalesa, Henry. (1994). *Success in Managing a Small Business.* Ashgate Publishing House, U.K.

Lang, James, R.; Calantone, Roger, J. and Gudmundson, Donald (1997). "Small Information seeking as a response to Environmental Threats and Opportunities". *Journal of Small Business* (January).

Lawrence, Peter and Mowbray, Melton (1985). "Small Business Breakthrough". *LAW*, USA. 1-17pp.

LeCornu, Mark. R.; Mc Mahon, Richard G.P.; Forsaith, David M. and Stanger, Anthory, M.J. (1996). "The Small Enterprise Financial objective Function". *Journal of Small Business Management.* USA. July.

Levin, R.I. and Travis, V.R. (1987). "Small Business Finance : What the Books Don't Say". *Harvard Business Review*, 65(6), 30-32.

Lewis, J. and Toon, K. (1986). *Accounting for Growth – Small Firm Growth and the Accounting Profession.* The Small Business Research Trust, U.K.

Lin, Engming (1980). "Inventory Control Systems for Small Business". *American Journal of Small Business Management*, USA. April. Vol. IV, No. – 4 Spring (April-June).

Linowes, Richard G. and Dixon, Bruce. R. (1992). "Small Business Management Development for a newly deregulated economy : The case of New Zealand'. *Journal of Small Business Management* (USA) Oct.

Luoma, G.A. (1967). *Accounting Information in Managerial Decision Making for Small and Medium Manufacturers.* Research Monograph No. 2. New York. National Association of Accounts, New York.

Lyles, M.A.; Baird, I.S.; Orris, J.B. and Kuratk (1993). "Formalised Planning in Family Owned Business : Increasing Strategic Choices". *Journal of Family Owned Business Management*; April. pp. 38-50.

Lynch, Richard. M. and Williamson, Robert. W. (1994). *Accounting for Management (Planning and Control).* Tata McGraw – Hill Publishing Ltd. New Delhi.

Lyneh, Richard. M. and Williamson, Robert. W. (1994). *Accounting for Management (Planing and Control).* Tata McGraw Hill Publishing House, New Delhi.

Mali, D.D. and Deka, P. (1995). *New Industrial Policy for Village and Small Enterprise.* Ed. Omsons Publication, New Delhi.

Mathur, S.P. (1979). *Economics of Small Scale Industries.* Sandeep Prakashan, Delhi.

Maurya, O.P. (2001). "Economics of Micro Enterprises". *Employment News*, Vol. XXV No. 41. 6-12 Jan.

Mayo, H. and Rosenbloom, B. (1975). "Ratio Analysis for the Small Businessman". *Journal of Small Business Management*, 13 (1), 19-11.

Mc Mahon, R.G.P. (1986). *Financial Management for Small Business.* CCH, Australia.

Mc Mahon, R.P.G. and Davies, L.G. (1991). *Financial reporting and analysis in Small Growth Enterprises : Evidence on practice in the North-East England.* Accounting and Finance Research Paper, The Flinder's University, South Australia.

McMahon, R.P.G. and Davies, L.G. (1994). "Financial reporting and analysis practices in Small Enterprises : Their association with growth rate and financial performance". *Journal of Small Business*, USA. Vol. 32. No. 1-4.9.

Meenakshisundaram, N. (2002). *Financial Management in Small Enterprises.* Kanishka Publishers, Distributors. New Delhi.

Meigs, Meigs, Bettner and Whittington (1996). *Accounting : The basis for Business Decisions.* McGrow Hill, U.S.A.

Meredith, G.G. (1986). *Financial Management of the Smaller Enterprise.* Mc Graw Hill, Sydney, Australia.

Merz, Russell, G.; Weber, Patricia, B. and Laetz, Virginia, B. (1994). "Linking Small Business Management with Entrepreneurial growth". *Journal of Small Business Management*, USA (Oct.).

Miller, H. and F. Kirschstein (1988). "Strategic Considerations for Promoting Micro-Enterprise in Developing Countries : A Role for Higher Education

Institutions", *International Review of Education*, 34 (Autumn), 495-499.

Mirza, A.M. (1979). "Budgeting : A versatile management tool for Small Business". *The Chartered Accountant in Australia.* August.

Mirza, A.M. (1979). "Budgeting : A Versatile Management Tool for Small Business". *The Chartered Accountant in Australia,* August.

Musheshwari, Dr. S.N. (1994). *Financial Management : Principles and Practices.* Sultan Chand & Sons, New Delhi.

Myddelton, R. Dr. (1997). *The Essence of Financial Management.* Prentice Hall of India Pvt. New Delhi.

Naffziger, D.W.; Hornsby, J.S. and Kuratko, D.F. (1992). "A Model of Entrepreneurial Motivation". Emerging Entrepreneurial Strategies in the 1990's : Proceedings of the 7th Annual Conference of the United States Association for Small Business and Enterprenurship. Chicago, III Ed. D.J. Naffziger and J.S. Hornsby. Muncie, Ind. Ball State University, 12-23.

Narayana, S.V. Dr.; Saha, S.; Ahmed, Taussif Dr. and Mehani, M.P. (1987). "Small Business-Financial Practices and Sticky Accounts". *Indian Journal of Commerce.* Vol. XL Parts 1 and 2 Nos. 150 and 151 January-June.

National Productivity Council (NPC) Research Division (1995). "Small Section in India : Role and Performance". *Productivity,* April-June, Vol. 36, No. 1.

National Productivity Council (NPC) Research Division (1995). *Productivity,* New Delhi. Vol. 36. No. 1. April-June.

National Sample Survey Organisation (NSS) (5th Round) (1998). *Small Trading Units in India and Their Basic Characteristics : 1997.* Department of Statistics, Government of India. December, 1998.

Nayak, A. and Greenfield, S. (1994). *The use of management accounting information for management for managing micro business.* Routledge, USA.

Neck, P.A. (1977). *Small Enterprise Development : Policies and Programmes.* International Labour Office, Geneva, Switzerland.

Odaka, Konosuke and Sawai, Nirora (1990). *Introduction to Small Business in Historical Perspective.* Printice Hall, U.K.

Osteryoung, Jerome.; Constand, Richard. L. and Nast, Donald (1992). "Financial Ratios in Large Public and Small Private Firms". *Journal of Small business Management* (USA) July.

Pandey, I.M. (1995). *Financial Management.* Vikash Publishing House Pvt. Ltd., New Delhi.

Pandey, J. and Tewary, N.B. (1979). "Locus of·Control and Achievement Values of Entrepreneurs" *Journal of Occupational Psychology.* 52, 107-111.

Perry, C. (1980). *A Small Business Model for Australian Policy Makers.* Working Paper, Queensland, Australia : Queensland Institute of Technology

Peters, Thomas, J. and Waterman, Robert. H. (1994). *In Search of Excellence.* Harper Collins Publisher, India.

Petty, J. W. and Bygrave, W.D. (1993). "What Does Finance have to say to the Enterprencur ?" *The Journal of Small Business Finance* 2(2), 125-137.

Petty, J.W. (1991). "Research in Small Firm Entrepreneurial Finance : A Note on Developing a Paradigm". *The Journal of Small Business Finance* 1(1), 89-90.

Pickle, Hal. B. and Abrahamson, Royce L. (1990). *Small Business Management.* John Wiley and Son. USA.

Pinson, Linda and Jinnett, Jeray (1989). *Keeping the Books – Basic Record keeping and Accounting for the Small Business.* Upstart Publishing Company Ltd.

Pinson, Linda and Jinnett, Jerry. (1989). *Keeping the Books.* Upstart Publishing Company, U.K.

Potts, A.J. (1992). "A study of success and failure rates of Small Business and the use or non – use of Accounting Information". Ph.D. Thesis, Geroge Washington University, Washington D.C. (USA).

Ramkrishna, K.J. (1962). *Financing for Small Scale Industries in India.* Asia Publishing House, Bombay.

Rao, Mohana, P. and Pramanik, Kumar, Alok (1996). *Current issues in Management Accounting.* Deep and Deep Publications. New Delhi.

Rao, Mohana. P. and Pramonik, Kumar Alok (1996). *Current issues in Management Accounting.* Deep and Deep Publication, New Delhi.

Rao, Mohona. P. (1999). *Financial Management (New Methods and Practices).* ed. Deep and Deep Publication, New Delhi.

Rao, P. Subba (1984). "New dimension of Indian Banking vis-à-vis Social Responsibilities of Commercial Banks". *The Indian Journal of Commerce,* Vol. XXXVII, Jan- March.

Rausch, E.N. (1982). "Financial Management for Small Business". *AMACON,* New York.

Ray, G.H. and Hutchinson, P.J. (1983). *The financing and financial control of Small Enterprise Development.* Gower Publishing, U.K.

Reid, Gavin. C. (1993). *Small Business Enterprise : An economic analysis.* Routledge, U.K.

Rice, George H. and Hamilton, Richard E. (1979). "Decision Theory and the Small Businessman". *American Journal of Small Business.* (USA) Vol. IV No. I. July.

Riggs, Walter. E. and Bracker, Jeffrey, S. (1986). "Operations Management and Financial Performance". *American Journal of Small Business.* (winter). Jan – March.

Roy, Hiranmoy; Das, Ashim Kumar and Rakshit, Sudipa (2003). "Importance of Entrepreneurship Awareness". *Journal of the North-Eastern Council, Shillong,* Vol. 23, No. 3, July-Sept. 2003.

Rudramurthy, D.G. (1997). "Institutional finance for the development of Small Scale Industries in Karnataka". Ph.D. Thesis (abstracted). Karnataka University.

Rue, Leslie. W. and Ibrabim, Nabil, A. (1998). "The

Relationship between Planning Sophistication and Performance in Small Business." *Journal of Small Business Management* (USA) Oct.

Rue, Leslie. W. and Ibrabim, Nabil. A. (1998). "The Relationship between Planning sophistication and performance in Small Businesses". *Journal of Small Business Management*, October.

Sarder, Jahangir Hossain, Ghosh, Dipak and Rosa, Peter (1997). "The Importance of support services to Small Enterprise in Bangladesh". *Journal of Small Business Management.* USA. April.

Satyanarayan, T. (1989). *Financing of Small Scale Industries.* Himalaya Publishing House, Bombay.

Scarborough, N.M. and Zimmerer, T.W. (1993). *Effective Small Business Management.* Macmillon Publishing Com. USA.

Schwenk, C.R. and Sharder, C.B. (1993). "Effects of Formal Strategic Planning on Financial Performance in Small Firms : A Meta-Analysis". *Enterpreneurship Theory and Practice* (Spring) 53-64.

Sen, Dilip Kumar, Jain, Sugan, C. and Bala, Swapan Kumar (2001). "Financial Management Tools : A Brief Study of their applicability in the changing industrial Environment of Bangladesh". *Journal of Accounting and Finance.* Vol. 16. No. 1. Oct. – 2001 – March – 2002.

Sengupta, Kumar Sankar and Kumar, Suraj (1996). "Significance of MIS in the Dynamics of Today's Organization with Particular Reference to Financial Control : An Overview". Ed. Rao, Mohana. P. and Pramonik, Kumar, Alok. *Current issues in Management Accounting.* Deep and Deep Publication, New Delhi. pp. 166-179.

Sharma, A.K. (1976). *Management Problems of Small Industries in Assam.* Ph.D. Thesis (unpublished), Gauhati University.

Sharma, D.D., Dhameja, S.K. and Gurjar, B.R. (1999).

Entrepreneurship strategic management and globalization. Rawat Publication, New Delhi.

Sharma, Madhav, Miller, Harry, G. and Reeder, Ronald (1990). "Micro Enterprise growth : Operational models and implementation assistance in third and fourth world countries". *Journal of Small Business Management,* USA. October.

Sharma, N.K. (2003). *Financial Accounting and Appraisal.* ABD Publishers, Jaipur.

Sharma, Subhash and Vithal, M.P. (1989). *Financial Accounting for Management.* Macmillan Indian Ltd., New Delhi.

Shergill, G.S. and Sarkaria, M.S. (1999). "Impact of Industry Type and Firm Characteristics on firm-level Financial Performance – Evidence from Indian Industry". *The Journal of Enterpreneurship.* Saga Publication, New Delhi.

SIDIBI Report on Small Scale Industries Sector-1999.

Sikidar, Sujit and Nath, Ghanashyam (2002). *Book-keeping and Accountancy* (Vol. I). Adhunik Prakashan, Guwahati. pp. 6-7.

Simon, Herbert, A. (1964). "On the concept of Organisation's roal". *Administrative Science Quarterly.* Vol. 9, No. 1 (June) 1-22.

Siop, Paulina and Ahmed, Kamran (2000). "The use of accounting information by Small Enterprise owner/ manager in emerging economies : The ease for Papua, New-Guinea". *Journal of Accounting and Finance.* Vol. 4. No. 2. Sept. 41-45.

Siropolis, Nicholas (1998). *Entrepreneurship and Small Business.* Indian Publishers and Distributors, Chennai, India.

Smith, Joan (1997). "Evaluation of Management and Marketing of Rotten Products in Assam". Ph.D. Thesis (unpublished), Natural Resources Institute, The University of Manitobe, Canada.

Smith, Ken. G.; Gannon, Martin J., Grimm, Curtis and Mitchell, Terence, R. (1988). "Decision Making Behavior in Smaller Entrepreneural and larger professionally managed firms". *Journal of Business Venturing.* Vol. 3. pp. 223-232. USA.

Soral, G. and Jain, Sudha (1994). "Management Accounting in Small Business : A case of Study". *Management Accounting.* Vol. 29. No. 11. 818-821.

Stanworth, M.J.K. and Curran, J. (1976). "Growth and the Small Firm - An Alternative View". *Journal of Management Studies.* Vol. 13, No. 2, May, USA.

Steinhoff, Dan (1978). *Small Business Management Fundamentals.* McGraw Hill Book company, USA.

Stepanek, Joseph, E. (1960). "*Managers of Small Industry* (An International Study)". Standford Research Institute, California, USA.

Storey, D.J. (1995). *Understanding the Small Business Sector.* Routledge, London.

T. Soon (1979). *Small Enterprises in Developing Countries : Care Studies and Conclusions.* London : IT Publication.

Tendler, J. (1987). "What ever Happened to Poverty Alleviation ?" *A Report of the Ford Foundation's Programs on Livelihood, Employment and Income Generation.* New York : Ford Foundation.

Terry, George, R. and Franklin, Stephen, G. (1997). *Principles of Management.* AITBS Publishers and Distributors, Delhi.

Thomas, J. and Evanson, R.V. (1987). "An Empirical Investigation of Association between Financial Ratio Use and Small Business Success". *Journal of Small Business Finance and Accounting,* 14(4), 555-571.

Tungale, L.A. (1952). "Financial Management for the Small Business". *Chapman and Grimes,* Inc. Boston.

Van Horne, James. C. and Wachowicz, Jr. John. M. (1996).

Fundamentals of Financial Management. Prentice Hall of India (P) Ltd., New Delhi.

Van Voorhis, K.R. (1981). "The DuPont Model Revisited : A simplified application of small business". *Journal of Small Business Management*, 18(4), 45-51.

Vepa, Ram. K. (1988). *Modern Small Industry in India – Problems and Prospects.* Saga Publication, New Delhi.

Vinayak, Rabinder (1987). "Financial Practices in Handloom Sector". *Indian Journal of Commerce*, Vol. XL. Parts. 1 and 2 Nos. 150 and 151. January-June. 120-121.

Vincent, Vern. C. (1996). "Decision-Making Policies Among Maxican – American Small Business Entrepreneurs". *Journal of Small Business Management*, USA. Oct.

Walker, E.W. and Petty, J.W. (1986). *Financial Management of the Small Firm.* (2nd edition). Prentice Hall, USA.

Watson, John and Everrett, Jim. E. (1996). "Do Small Businesses have high Failure Rates ?" *Journal of Small Business Management*, USA. Jan.

World Bank (1978). *Employment and Development of Small Enterprise.* Washington, D.C. : The World Bank.

Wrapp, H.E. (1967). "Good managers don't make policy decisions". *Harvard Business Review.* 45(5) : pp. 91-99.

Yusuf, A. (1995). "Critical success, factors for Small Business : Perception of South Pacific entrepreneurs". *Journal of Small Business Management*, Vol. 33. No. 2.

INDEX

❑❑❑